THE WAY OUT OF LONELINESS

THE WAY OUT OF LONELINESS

Joan Gibson

Gateway Books, Bath

First published in 1991
by GATEWAY BOOKS
The Hollies, Wellow,
Bath, BA2 8QJ

© *1991 by Joan Gibson*

cover artist: Paul Nelson
cover design: Studio B, Bristol

Set in 11/12½ pt. Sabon by
Ann Buchan (Typesetters), Middlesex
Printed by and bound by Hartnoll of Bodmin

British Library Cataloguing in Publication Data:
Gibson, Joan 1922–
The way out of loneliness
1. Loneliness
I. Title
158.2

ISBN 0-946551-69-3

Contents

Preface

It may be that you have picked up this book very doubt-fully, thinking that it is easy enough for someone to give glib advice on a problem like loneliness. I should like to emphasise that it is written from personal experience. I have been there too, and am convinced that the escape route described here is the most effective way of achieving liberation. It really does work.

Introduction – Your Passport

Loneliness. What a sad word this is. It is responsible for so much pain and misery; so many hours of weary boredom and hopelessness. If you are lonely now, existing rather than living, in a world which seems to be hurrying uncaringly by, leaving you a solitary onlooker, you will be only too well aware of this. Don't despair. There is a way out of loneliness; an escape route which you can discover and follow. It will take time, patience and much determination, but if you are sincere in your desire to free yourself from the chains of loneliness, you will be able to do so. You will achieve it by re-discovering the world.

This is not so strange a statement as may at first appear. You will have accomplished it at least twice before in your life. Consider the amazing, new world you encountered when, as a small child, you entered the realm of school. Novel experiences, one after the other, crowded upon you, and you were filled with awe and wonder at the sheer immensity of it all.

You re-discovered the world in a different way on the day you first fell in love, and again when you began your chosen career, or married life. These events have now, perhaps, dropped far back into the past, or have eluded you altogether, and your world has been slowly and imperceptibly growing smaller and more monotonous, until you have found yourself trapped in your dark, restricted prison of isolation and misery. It is time for you to escape from it and begin a new phase in your life. This book will help you to find the way out, and will lead you

3

along the path from loneliness to freedom in a new world.

You must decide, first of all, whether you are now prepared to embark on such a journey. Journeys can be long, tedious and tiring, and this will be no exception, but journeys bring us to the place where we wish to be. They are usually well worth the effort. What will this particular journey involve for you? You probably cannot change the circumstances which are causing your present loneliness, but you WILL be able to learn how to change yourself, your attitude to life, and your daily routine, and you will begin to move into new and unexplored territories.

This is less complicated than it sounds. Think back to yourself as a small child starting school. You were then in exactly the same situation. New things were presented to you. You did not know whether or not you would like them, but you had no choice. School attendance is mandatory, and so, at the age of five, is participation in all that is on the curriculum. Some lessons you certainly enjoyed more than others; some you actively disliked at first, then came to find pleasure in them. Your growing skills in reading, writing and number opened new doors for you, hitherto undreamed of. Through all your learning experiences you slowly matured, and life became fuller and more interesting. Each fresh discovery a child makes fills him with wonder and astonishment. There is no time for boredom.

To escape now from your state of loneliness you will need to go through a similar metamorphosis, and it is the purpose of this book to guide you, step by step, along the way. The rewards will be great, so do not be afraid to tackle it. Before you begin there are, of course, careful preparations to be made. No-one starts a journey without first thinking about the route, their own fitness, what they should take with them and so on.

We will begin by looking at a map of the way you will be travelling. It will be like a series of rooms, each one leading out of the next, and starting from the small room marked 'loneliness' in which you are now so unhappily imprisoned.

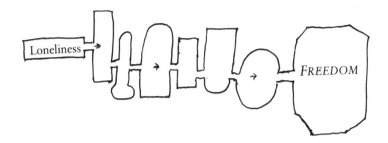

In order to reach freedom from loneliness it will be necessary to pass through and spend some time in each. You may find that you are unable to linger in some of the rooms, for reasons which I will explain later, and in this case you will have to remain for a longer period in subsequent ones.

The number of rooms will not be the same for everyone, indeed, there may be short cuts along the way, but these will not be marked on the map and will only become apparent later. As on any long journey, there will be hazards to avoid. In every room there will be possible discouragements which will tempt you to turn back and seek the refuge of your lonely prison. However, with courage and determination, it is certainly possible to overcome any obstacle that may present itself along the way. The remaining chapters of this book will be in the form of a guide, which will conduct you from room to room and will explain how you can travel safely through each, avoiding any potential pitfalls.

The time which you will spend on your journey will vary from person to person. If you are working during the day, you will only be able to travel in the evenings, or at weekends. Those who have all day on their hands will certainly have more time at their disposal, but because their loneliness is, perhaps, greater and they have become almost institutionalised in their tiny prison, it could well prove to be a longer journey for them. However, the escape route is possible for everyone.

You must now consider your health and strength, because this, too, will affect your travelling. You may have sight or hearing problems. Perhaps you are physically handicapped, or housebound through age or disability. Don't worry. When I said that some people would only be able to pass quickly through certain rooms, I was referring to those who have these sorts of problems. None will prevent them from making the journey, but, for them, there will be some modifications or special facilities which I will deal with in the guide book.

We now come to a most important item; your special 'passport', which you must keep with you at all times. It is an absolute necessity if you are to reach your desired destination, and I would recommend that you read it through every single day. It is, as you will see, in the form of a resolution, and perhaps some of its clauses may surprise you. Please read it through now and think about it. These are the aims you are going to carry with you and which will help you to emerge from your loneliness and unhappiness.

Finally, here are two more most important things which you must remember as you travel:

You must NOT look for friends.

You must NOT look for happiness.

You are probably surprised by this because, obviously, these are the very things you most wish to have. It is a strange fact of life that the more we search for happiness, the more it seems to elude us, and the same is true of friendship. Stop looking for them and, more often than not, they will creep up on you unawares. When people are very lonely they tend to latch on to others and cling to them in desperation, which has the effect of driving away potential friends. So, as you journey on, you will certainly encounter other travellers, and friendship may grow spontaneously, as I hope it will, but please remember that you must not, on any account, try to force it. Wait for it to come to you.

As I have already said, I am setting before you the plan of a journey that will take much time and patience. What

RESOLUTION

I .... hereby resolve that:

1. I will no longer feel that the world is a dull place, but I will set out to re-discover it.

2. I will not feel sorry for myself, for it is within my power to rebuild my life.

3. I will believe in myself, and learn to use to the full all the talents and abilities I have.

4. I will learn to enjoy my own thoughts and my own company.

5. I will find a way in which I can put something that is good and positive into the world.

6. I will not be discouraged by failures, but I will go on trying until I achieve something that is worthwhile.

7. Above all, I will resolve never to have a closed mind.

Today is the first day of the rest of my life.

you should do now, is to think about it, re-read the resolution, and then go carefully through the following pages of this book; your guide along the escape route. I hope you will then decide to set out on your pilgrimage of re-discovery, that you will find it an enjoyable and enlightening experience and that, at the end of it, you will know that you have, at last, put loneliness behind you for ever.

The First Door – Foreign Lands

The day has arrived on which you will start your journey. You know that it is going to bring about a major change in your life and, no doubt, you are feeling a little apprehensive; you have become so acclimatised to your own small dungeon of loneliness. Miserable as it has been, it has grown familiar, and the pattern of your days boringly predictable. Now all this is going to alter. Don't be concerned. You will progress only slowly, a step at a time, and you will be able to linger at each stage for as long as you wish, before going on to the next.

Be sure that you have your 'passport' with you as, with some trepidation, you open the tiny door leading out of your prison-house and emerge into the corridor. Immediately before you is a larger door, and on it a notice – 'FOREIGN LANDS'.

You may remember a poem by R.L. Stevenson, in which he imagined himself, as a small boy, climbing into the branches of a cherry tree, and so managing to see over the garden wall and into the larger world beyond. He dreamed of setting out along those alluring roads which stretched far into the distance, journeying ever on and on, reaching and crossing the mighty ocean; and of course, when he grew up, despite poor health, he did travel extensively and gained much pleasure from it. This room which you have now entered is going to take you into a foreign land; a land of your own choice and through which, like Stevenson, you will travel in imagination. As you journey you will doubtless be able to say, as he did, that you have discovered much of value, and found

> ". . . many pleasant places more
> that I have never seen before."

Childhood dreams are often realised. There is a famous picture of the boyhood of Raleigh. The lad is seated on the quay-side, listening enraptured to the stirring tales of an old sea-dog, and this may well have happened in real life, so firing his longing to explore for himself even stranger parts of the world.

When you were young you probably heard curious stories of other lands also, and wondered about them. It may not now be possible to go there in person, but much can be discovered by the armchair traveller. There are advantages too. You will not be plagued by mosquitoes if you visit the tropics, nor trapped by treacherous ice-floes in some Antarctic wilderness.

Your knowledge of the world, though, is likely to be only superficial at present. Could you, for example, on opening an atlas, immediately put your finger on Surinam, Puerto Rico, Haiti, the Aleutian Islands, Lake Eyre, Chad, Honshu, Bhutan, Laos, Corfu, or even the Isle of Arran? This will soon be remedied.

Without more ado then, you must open the door before you and enter the room. In the centre is a table, and on it various things which you will need; an atlas, coloured pens, notebooks, tracing paper, and a whole pile of books of various shapes and sizes.

Your first task is to take the atlas and open it at a map of the world. Now you must ask yourself which country, out of all those laid out before you, you would most like to visit if you had the opportunity. Perhaps you have been fascinated by the mysteries of the East, and would like to see the Great Wall of China or the Taj Mahal, the high peaks of the Himalayas or the strange land of Tibet. Maybe Africa appeals to you, with its wide, rolling plains and abundant wild life, or you might long to travel through America, or to explore Australia or New Zealand. There are wonders, too, not quite so far distant; the

Austrian forests and mountains, castles on the Rhine, the beautiful old cities of Italy, the ancient monuments of Greece, and the Holy Land with its wealth of Biblical history. The world holds so many contrasts; such extremes of climate, from sun-baked deserts to the icy wastes of the poles. You have a very wide choice, and your aim will be to take just one area which particularly interests you, and find out as much about it as you can.

You will, of course, have some general knowledge of it already, but you are now going to add to this in every way you can. Let us suppose that you have decided on Spain. You will need to draw maps and plans, and consult all the books you can find to help you to learn what the ordinary Spanish people do in both villages and towns, what they grow in the country, what work is carried on in the towns, how they spend their time and their money, their sports, their customs, their national dress and so on. Then the country itself must be considered. Where will you see mountains, rivers and lakes, what flowers grow there, and what sort of trees? Is it true that "the rain in Spain falls mainly on the plain", or is this just a myth? What animals would you expect to find, both wild and domestic, and what is the climate like throughout the year? Are some places more suitable for holidays than others? How has the tourist industry affected Spain? You must certainly also consider Spanish history. Everyone knows about the Armada, but there have been a great many more interesting events in Spain's past, and you will need to find out about the present political situation there. Spanish artists and explorers are well worth investigating too, and so are the lovely Spanish dances, their colourful festivals, and their passion for bull fighting. Books of travel in Spain are numerous and very varied and, by reading these, you will unearth all sorts of interesting legends, and fragments of knowledge that were previously unknown to you. There is no need to concentrate on serious reading only. You will find many books of adventure or romance in the fictional section of the library.

This is just to give you an example of the sort of

discovering you are going to do, whichever country you happen to choose. Decide to spend a short time each day working on it. Obviously, it will take a long while to cover all the ground I have suggested, but set aside anything from half an hour to two hours as your daily discovering period.

You are going to require certain basic materials, and your first priority will be a good atlas. You may already possess one, but do remember that the world has changed a great deal in recent years; many countries and towns now have new names, and frontiers have been moved. A modern atlas is certainly a most useful possession and, if it is easily accessible, you will be able to look up places mentioned in the newspapers or on television news bulletins, thus gradually becoming more knowledgeable about the world in general.

However, your chosen 'foreign land' is the main thing on which to concentrate at present and, as a preliminary step, it will be helpful to trace this carefully from your atlas, filling in the main rivers and towns, and colouring mountains and lakes. Greaseproof paper serves quite adequately for tracing. The completed map will go on the first page of your book of notes, where it will be your task to record all the interesting discoveries that you make.

You will need to refer constantly to various kinds of books, so a visit to the library is now indicated. I would suggest that you start in the children's section, where there will be elementary facts about your country and, perhaps, stories of explorers, customs and legends to get you off the mark. Try to find out about the national flag, the country's patron saint and so on. *The Children's Encyclopaedia* and *The Encyclopaedia Britannica* are both good sources of knowledge, and will be in the Reference Section.

Look among school text-books on bookshelves and, if you live within travelling distance of London, do visit Foyle's Bookshop in Charing Cross Road; a real Aladdin's cave of books of every sort. From elementary books you can progress to more advanced reading in the adult library. Many books have appended lists of suggestions for further reading, so that one source of enquiry may well lead you on to another. Keep in mind that librarians will always try to obtain a book for you if it is not on their shelves.

Apart from books there are other possible areas to investigate. How much produce from your chosen country can you find in the shops? Make lists of this. Some of the larger supermarkets stock exotic fruits and vegetables from all over the world and, of course, manufactured goods originate from almost any country you can name. Do not overlook the special charity shops, such as those run by OXFAM, which have a variety of handicrafts from the Third World. Try to find, and if possible build up a collection of as many articles as you can from your particular country. Obtain the OXFAM catalogue and look through it carefully for ideas. Make a scrapbook of food labels, or a small album of stamps, and look out for dolls dressed in national costume. Better still, as these are usually quite expensive, make your own little doll, using a picture of the national dress for guidance. As your discovering proceeds, you will be able to continue along whichever lines appeal to you the most.

You will see that there is ample to occupy your time, and plenty of choice in the various mediums. That is why this room makes an ideal starting point. The work you are going to tackle is not too difficult or demanding, and it can be done when and how you choose.

At this stage I should point out that if you have poor eyesight, and would find reading, map drawing etc. a problem, you are permitted to pass quickly through the first room and concentrate instead on *ROOM no. 2*.

For everyone else, I must now warn you of some pitfalls to avoid. In every room you will find lurking a gremlin who is eager to discourage you. He is sure to put these doubts and objections into your mind. Be prepared and ready to answer him back.

Gremlin: "You are not really interested in all this!"
ANSWER: That is quite true. If you had been, you would have already been working on it. However, you are aiming to awaken a new interest as time goes by.

Gremlin: "It's too much like school."

ANSWER: No, it is very different. YOU are making the choices as to what you will study and for how long. You will be given no examinations or tests. You can work at your own pace and in your own way.

Gremlin: "What's the point?"

ANSWER: You are going to escape from loneliness by building up your knowledge. You are going to make yourself more confident and an altogether more interesting person. You are going to widen your horizons and change your whole attitude to life.

Gremlin: "You are hopeless at drawing maps and making notes."

ANSWER: Perhaps you are, but it doesn't matter. They are not going to be marked or assessed. The maps and notes are for your benefit only. You will gain satisfaction from doing them as well as you can, but there is no-one to judge them but yourself.

Answer the gremlin back firmly, and treat his suggestions with contempt. Tell him you have no intention of abandoning your quest at this early stage. Read through those resolutions in your 'passport', then settle down to spend a little time each day on the study of your 'foreign land'. Try to vary the work so that it is absorbing and enjoyable; some written notes, some reading.

Then, in a week or so, when you have made a good start and are used to this daily routine, you will be ready to look for new interests, and to progress to the next stage of your journey.

You must now leave *ROOM 1* and walk to the door marked '2', on which you will find the notice '*HOME-GROUND*'. Open the door and enter.

The Second Door – Home-Ground

When you enter *ROOM 2* you will find only a single item on the table before you: a street plan of your own town, city or village. Everything else you will require must be sought out of doors.

How well do you know your home territory? This will depend partly on the length of time you have lived there but, even if you have been acquainted with the area all your life, there are sure to be some aspects of it that are still unfamiliar. These you will be searching out.

When I was young, the custom of taking a daily walk was quite commonplace. Nowadays, we rarely leave the house unless we have some specific objective in view; shopping, going to work, meeting a friend and so on. The only people who simply go for walks appear to be those who have to exercise their dogs. This, I feel, is to be regretted. Going for a walk was a marvellous pastime, a stress reducer and a sure source of interest. It was preferable to take a companion, if possible, in order to share leisurely conversation on the way, but solitary walks could be almost equally enjoyable.

In those days, most people, young or old, would carry walking-sticks. Not only were these a help when the way grew weary, but they were invaluable in dealing with troublesome nettles or brambles, securing a succulent blackberry from the top of the hedge, or fending off a less than friendly dog. I feel it regrettable that, nowadays, they are considered suitable only as a prop for the extremely elderly or infirm.

14

You are going to be setting out on many excursions from this room so, despite the walking stick's fall from popularity, I do recommend your taking one along with you. If nothing else, it will be a deterrent against muggers! It's optional, of course, and entirely up to you, but I should be happy to see them come back into favour. Always choose a stout stick, with a curved handle that will fit comfortably into your palm, and ensure that it is tipped with a rubber ferrule, so that it will not slip when you put your weight on it. I have quite a few walking-sticks at home. The handle of one was carved by my grandfather in the shape of a snake's head, with the tail curling down the stick itself; a real work of art. In those days, shepherds often fashioned their own crooks, and very beautiful they were. However, to return to your proposed walks. Before setting out you will need to plan the route.

If you live in a town, you will be very familiar with the main streets, the shopping areas, and buildings such as pubs, churches, schools and cinemas. Whole new estates, however, are constantly springing up, old buildings being demolished, and blocks of flats erected on any available space. It is difficult to remember the location of newer streets when someone asks for directions. How many times a name will seem vaguely familiar, but you find yourself quite unable to place it. By regularly consulting the road map when planning your walks, you will soon be well qualified as a guide to your area. You will quickly learn which roads are cul-de-sacs, and which will give you a short cut from one district to another. Be sure to try out all the interesting little alley ways or footpaths, which so often link up various parts of the town. What is your local name for these? They are twittens in parts of the South, lonnings or wynds in the North, closes in Scotland, and I am sure there must be many more equally pleasing variations in between.

A profusion of street names will not worry you if you live in a village, but even here, you have probably left many of the smaller footpaths and lanes unexplored. Never neglect a footpath; they are always worth following.

I came upon a heronry once, when passing a little copse which edged a farm track. The young birds were beginning to hatch, and were being guarded by one sentinel heron perched high in the tallest tree. His harsh warning cries drew my attention, and I saw one of the parent birds returning with food, skimming over the wood, legs trailing and head held high, like a galleon in full sail. I was so glad I had taken that path.

Look for footpaths on your map. They are not always easy to trace on the ground, unless you are quite certain which direction they will take. They usually start off plainly signposted and well-trodden, and you set out confidently, only to find yourself presently stranded in the middle of a field, with no indication of which way to go next! Luckily, in our country, civilisation is never too far away, so getting lost is seldom a disaster.

If you are thoroughly familiar with your own village, try going a little further afield. Walking in the country is seldom without its rewards; there are rare wild flowers to discover, bounty like nuts and blackberries or even strawberries to gather from the hedgerows; rabbits, squirrels, birds and butterflies to catch your attention, and young creatures to observe on the farms. It is a thrill to see the first swallow of summer, to hear the cuckoo, watch rooks following the plough, or to find an unexpected carpet of bluebells in the woods.

Towns can still offer you glimpses of wild life in the parks, but in addition there is much more to engage your interest. Because the town will cover a large area, it is best to start with the streets nearest to your home, and when you have thoroughly explored these, then to venture further afield. You will probably have a range of shops which you usually patronise for your day to day needs. Experiment now with others. If you normally shop in the supermarket, switch to smaller stores for a while, or vice versa. Spend time in window-shopping, instead of just hurrying through the purchase of a list of your usual provisions. Look for new foods which you have not previously tried.

We can so easily become boringly conservative in our tastes and unwilling to experiment with anything at all unusual. This is frequently the attitude of young children, who will say, 'I don't like that', before even tasting it, simply because it is unfamiliar to them. In recent years there has been a much wider range of foods in the shops, so don't be afraid to sample them.

How often, I wonder, do you indulge in having a meal out? This need not be outrageously extravagant if you go to a pub, small cafe, or sandwich bar. Perhaps you could make this a weekly event, trying as many new places as possible, or buying a take-away meal. It all makes for variety, though once you have found a favourite establishment, you will probably choose to go there regularly. If you dislike having meals out, or are on a very tight budget, try instead to find a place for morning coffee or an afternoon cup of tea.

Towns have so many other attractions, in addition to shops, pubs and restaurants. Look out for markets, exhibitions, jumble sales, or car boot sales. Charities often hold 'coffee mornings', and these can be quite enjoyable. Watch for notices of any local meetings. There are sure, too, to be many clubs and associations in the neighbourhood catering for all tastes. These would include social gatherings, musical groups, clubs for philately, bridge, scrabble, darts and so on. You will be able to find out details of these by enquiring at your library.

The important thing is, not only to be able to find your way about your town and be aware of all it can offer, but also to know its history. If there is a local history association, this is well worth joining, as, through it, you will be able to learn about buildings of historical interest in your area, famous characters of centuries gone by who were born there, or had some connection with it, and whether your town has exciting stories in its past or any other claim to fame. Your reference library will be certain to contain books of local happenings, and your town, if it has roots in the past, may even have its own museum. If so, you should definitely visit it.

It is surprising how many people are woefully ignorant about their home towns. This is, I think, especially true of those living in the large cities. Many a Londoner is unable to direct the foreign tourist to a particular historical site, or tell him the significance of a statue or monument. In the country, too, it is holiday-makers rather than the locals who are eager to climb the hills, or view spectacular waterfalls or caves. If we live in the area, we know that these sights are nearby and take them for granted, but seldom bother to visit them.

Your purpose, then, as you set out from this room, is to learn to know your own home-ground really well. You must resolve, each day, to go out on a brief tour of exploration. This will be in addition to any necessary shopping trips. Plan your route in advance, so that it will be as interesting as possible, and try to include some specific objective. You could, perhaps, look out for unusual house names, explore a footpath, feed the ducks on the pond, watch some sport in the park, or even just call at a cafe for a cup of tea or coffee.

If you find something worth bringing home with you, such as a beautiful leaf, a wild flower, or a curiously marked stone, you can start a collection of these. You may like to make a note of the number of different trees, birds, or wild flowers you can identify. Another variation is to take a short bus ride and then walk back.

Going for a walk will always bring added and unlooked-for bonuses. You can never predict what you may encounter on the way. Whether in town or country, the unexpected is sure to happen.

I once came across a troupe of morris dancers, and stopped to watch their performance. A quite different drama took place, when I saw a man snatch and make off with an old lady's purse in a crowded supermarket. Others chased him, in hot pursuit, the thief was cornered, and the handbag returned to its tearful owner; quite an exciting episode, and totally unforeseen.

Sometimes wild animals or birds will provide us with great pleasure. I offered some pieces of biscuit to squirrels in the park one day, and was delighted when they ventured quite close to me. One finally lost its fear sufficiently to take the food from my fingers, and it was heart-warming to feel those soft, small paws resting trustfully on my hand. On another occasion, I watched as a girl scattered some bread on the grass for the birds. A flock of gulls gathered, swirling round and round in a slowly descending spiral towards the ground. With the sun glinting on their beautiful white and silver wings, it was as graceful as a ballet.

I can remember once, when on a coach excursion, we were exploring the grounds of a stately home. A 'woodland walk' was sign-posted, but, as it was rather muddy, few of my fellow-travellers were inspired to try it. However, it was bluebell time, and I couldn't resist such an alluring path. At the edge of the wood was a stile, and the way continued through a field of long, wet grass beyond. It was when I was half way across this field, that I came face to face with a very large snake. I heard a loud hiss at my feet, and there it was; a grass snake, several feet long. I was delighted to have seen one at such close quarters, and said so to the other passengers when I returned. But most of them did not share my enthusiasm! One lady went quite white and said, "Thank God I didn't go along that path!" I thought it a pity that she felt like this, for grass snakes, though large, are quite harmless and, like all snakes, have the most beautiful eyes. However, meeting a snake is not an everyday occurrence, and was a novel experience for me.

From the examples I have given, you will see how easily, by just leaving the shelter of your own four walls, you can, with very little effort, make your life more interesting. But we have to keep ourselves on the alert. All kinds of events are happening around us and, by keeping our eyes and ears open, we shall find much to observe and learn. Do not allow yourself to become cynical and disillusioned with ordinary living. Even the humblest leaf or flower is a miracle of perfection, beauty and wonder. Try, like Blake, to see,

"A World in a grain of sand,
And a Heaven in a wild flower."

What you are aiming to do is to bring back with you from your walk a picture in your mind of something that will encourage and inspire you. For instance, on a brief shopping trip this morning, I can recall seeing a single rose, perfect in form, its petals folded back to reveal glowing tones of soft peach and gold. A little further along the road, where for a while had stood the sad, jagged stump of an elm tree, felled by recent storms, I saw that this had now sent out a new and vigorous growth which, though the tree, lacking its main branches, had a curious, bush-like shape, was strong and flourishing; a triumph of life over apparent death.

You will have realised that your activities from *ROOM 1*, where you will be studying a foreign land, are going to be very different from your excursions into your own environment from *ROOM 2*. This is as it should be. You will now have two contrasting assignments to engage in each day. Going out of the house is extremely important. It is all too easy, especially if you are inclined to be reserved, to shut yourself away from others, and this is never advisable. Human beings are gregarious animals, and need to be in contact with each other. This is not to say that we must constantly be involved in noisy parties and social gatherings. As sheep or cows in a field, it will often suffice just to be within sight and sound of others. Simply observing our fellow creatures can be fascinating in itself.

In the days when Lyons Corner Houses were scattered about London, these made convenient meeting places; an alternative to waiting under the clock at Waterloo Station. I often met a friend at the Piccadilly Corner House and, if she happened to be late, I was quite happy to pass the time watching the amazing variety of people who passed through its doors. It seemed as though representatives from every imaginable corner of the earth, and from every walk of life, would assemble there. It is equally illuminating to watch the crowds on a main line railway station, as they hurry about their business. It is good to build up our powers of observation for, as has been wisely said, "the proper study of mankind is man".

When you set out each day on your tour of exploration, you will have ample opportunities for observation. Choose something to study in depth: flowers, birds, trees, architecture, or whatever you are likely to come across easily when you are out.

Here, then, is the new daily task to add to your *ROOM 1* assignment. Where you will go, and the nature of your investigations will be your decision; but even if you can only spend a short time on each, these two activities must now form part of your daily routine.

It is inevitable that, at this point, the gremlin of *ROOM 2* will make his presence felt.

Gremlin: "You already know everything about this place and, in any case, you couldn't care less."

ANSWER: This is an extremely doubtful statement. There is always more to discover. Think of it as a challenge to find out new facts. When I lived near London, a French pen-friend came to stay and I discovered, to my shame, that she, because she had taken the trouble to study the subject beforehand, knew more of London than I did, and was able to direct me to places in the City she wished to visit.

Gremlin: "The weather is too bad for you to go out today."

ANSWER: If you have warm, waterproof clothing, then it is not. Fresh air and exercise in moderation are always beneficial. Should the weather be really unpleasant, you need only go for a short distance, but you SHOULD make some attempt. If you own a dog, you will, in any case, need to exercise him daily, whatever the weather.

Gremlin: "You are too tired today."

ANSWER: Mental tiredness needs physical exercise to ease it, and you are unlikely to be physically tired if you have been indoors for most of the day. However, you can make your walk a short one if you really do feel fatigued. It is up to you to regulate the distance you go. Keep long explorations for the days when you have the most energy.

Gremlin: "It would be nicer to stay indoors by the fire."

ANSWER: No doubt it would, but it will be even nicer and much more enjoyable to look forward to that warm fire and hot meal as a reward for your efforts when you return home.

Gremlin: "You already have quite enough to do."

ANSWER: Nonsense! To be fully occupied is the best way to defeat loneliness, and this is the whole object of your endeavours.

If, despite your efforts to silence him, the gremlin is still half convincing you to give up, try reading through your 'passport' once more. Besides, you do not yet know what lies ahead of you in ROOM 3. This may be of a less arduous nature. Before you go further, though, give yourself time to get well into the way of your daily discoveries on your home-ground.

When this is firmly established, you may carry on to door 3. On it you will find the notice, 'SELF-CARE.'

The Third Door – Self-Care

As you open the door of *ROOM 3*, you will meet with a surprise. Every wall consists of mirrors, so that wherever you turn you will see your own reflection. Here your attention is going to be focussed upon yourself, and you will be investigating your image as you see yourself, and as others see you. You will be learning how best to treat and to look after yourself.

If you are elderly, disabled, or agoraphobic, you may have been able to linger only briefly in *ROOM 2*; if your eyesight is poor, you will have been excused from much of the work in *ROOM 1*, but *ROOM 3* is for everyone.

When we live alone, we often feel tempted to neglect our appearance. We feel that, because we have only ourselves to consider, we need take no pains to dress neatly or tidy our hair. A man, if he is going to remain indoors, may not trouble to shave; a woman may feel it easier to wander round the house in a dressing gown and bedroom slippers. It is so easy to let standards slip, and once we do, we tend to make less and less effort as time goes by. The housework gets neglected, we make do with skimpy meals, and find ourselves becoming progressively more apathetic and slipshod. We fall into the way of thinking, 'No-one else sees or cares, so what does it matter?' This attitude is wrong. We have to matter to ourselves, and we need to re-build our self-esteem. We cannot expect others to think us worth befriending, if we have such a low opinion of our own value and place in society. We must get out of the habit of feeling, 'It's only for me, so it doesn't matter.' It is not conceit to see ourselves as deserving of equal respect and consideration as others.

If we live alone it is, in fact, even more important that we should like ourselves. We have to accept ourselves as we are, for although it is possible to change attitudes, habits and conduct to some extent, we cannot, and indeed should not wish to, change our basic personality. This is what makes us the unique being we are. That human being will remain with us throughout our lives, so we might as well come to terms with our strengths and weaknesses, short-comings and talents, and make the best possible use of them. Never feel you should apologise for being yourself. "It's only me", is an altogether wrong approach.

Now is the time to take stock of yourself. Have a good look in one of those mirrors. What do you see? No doubt you would like to discover a slender sylph or a virile Adonis reflected there. That, alas, is unlikely to be the case. Handsome youths and beautiful maidens are comparatively rare. Yet, how dull the world would be if they were commonplace! Good looks are not vital or even important. The most unattractive of mortals still find happiness and fulfilment in life. The qualities we need are not such transient ones.

What, then, does the mirror reveal? A middle-aged lady, perhaps, with a lined face and greying hair, or a rather dumpy girl with a hopeless expression, a balding gentleman with a little too much weight below the belt, or a gangling lad, thin and pale, looking, as my country-born mother used to say, like a 'yard of pump water'. Whatever the image, this is YOU. You are looking at a true picture of yourself; you, as you are presenting yourself to the world. If the picture does not satisfy you, then now is the time to do something about it. While you are in this room, you will learn how to set about this. We will consider various ways of improving your image.

1. POSTURE

The school I attended when I was young still retained some rather out-moded Victorian ideologies, one of which was an insistence on a correct posture. We were awarded good or bad 'posture marks', which were entered on our House records. Woe betide those who slouched when walking, lolled on a desk, or shuffled their feet. We found it somewhat irksome, but posture IS important. The way we stand, walk and sit has a direct effect on our health. Poor posture can bring about back pain, aching joints and a stiff neck, or may aggravate digestive and chest troubles. A health treatment known as the Alexander Technique was devised based entirely on correcting posture, and those who teach it claim that it can greatly improve our well-being.

The Victorians would practise walking with a large book balanced on their heads, in order to achieve an erect carriage, or they would lie down on a board or other rigid surface to ensure a straight back. There is no need for us to go to such extremes, but we should try to follow these rules:

Walking

a. Don't always look on the ground as you walk. This may lead to your discovering the odd coin or so, but it gives you a dejected air and eventually makes you feel that way. Unless the ground is so uneven that you need to watch your feet, look around and ahead of you as you go along.

b. Brisk walking is less tiring and better for your health than a slow amble. It is all right to wander aimlessly occasionally, but your normal walking pace should be purposeful and steady.

c. Try not to hump up your shoulders when you walk. Keep them relaxed.

d. Do not let your head poke forward. Walk and stand tall.

Sitting

a. Never sit on the extreme edge of a chair.

b. Avoid crossing your legs or twisting them round the

chair legs. It is, however, permissible to cross your feet at the ankles.

c. If you are typing or working at a table for any length of time, make sure that your chair is the right height, so that your back is well supported, your legs can reach the floor, and you are as comfortable as possible.

Standing

It is always tiring and puts a strain on your legs if you stand for too long, but if this is unavoidable it sometimes helps to lift your heels from the ground slightly and lower them again from time to time. Keep your weight balanced equally between both legs.

Check in the mirror that you are standing or sitting correctly now. Notice how much better you look when you are standing upright instead of slouching, or sitting in a relaxed manner, rather than lolling in the chair or perching on the edge of it.

The mirrors round the room will help you to check your posture now and again, until it comes naturally to you to assume a correct carriage. A word of warning may be necessary. You must avoid walking in a stiff and rigid manner, as if you had forgotten to remove the hanger from your clothes. Allow yourself to relax. An example of perfect posture may be seen in the dignified walk of most Indian women who seem to possess a natural grace of movement. This is why the sari, their national dress, can seldom be worn with such elegance by a European. African women, too, because of their practice of carrying heavy objects on their heads, are able to walk with this same dignity and confidence.

2. HAIR

Consider now the state of your hair. Are you completely satisfied with it? Hair has, from earliest times, had an important part to play in shaping personality. We tend to form our first impressions of a person by looking at their hair. Styles have changed dramatically down the ages, but in these days length, colour and shaping are matters of individual choice. Long hair in a man was once a sign of virility, though now the same is often attributed to baldness. A woman's hair was, in past centuries, regarded as her 'crowning glory', and she would endeavour to grow it long enough to sit upon. Today, hair still helps to indicate personality, so if we want to alter ourselves in any way, this will be an obvious starting point. You wish to change from being lonely and dissatisfied with your way of life, therefore, start by considering your hair.

On looking back over my life I can see, rather to my surprise, that whenever I have changed my hair style, I have subsequently increased my own self-confidence, and tackled new ventures. During my early years at school I had long pigtails, the ends of which the boys who sat behind me took great pleasure in dipping in ink wells. I held a low opinion of boys in those days! I progressed to a short bob when attending the grammar school, then to a pony tail on starting my first job. I was very shy and withdrawn in my pony tail days, but during the war the fashion of wearing one's hair up in a roll round the head became popular. Once I had adopted this, I felt really adult and sophisticated, and acted accordingly. In my mother's time, a girl 'put her hair up' as a sign that she had left her childhood firmly behind her, in much the same way as a wealthier young lady would be presented at Court, or would be given a 'coming out' party or ball.

There is no reason at all why you should not now move into a similarly momentous phase in your life. Changes can be made at any age, and an alteration in hair style, however slight, can mark its beginning. It need be nothing more than adding a coloured slide or comb, changing the position of the parting, using a colour rinse, or having a shorter cut. Alternatively, you may like to try a completely new style, or even experiment with a wig to wear on special occasions.

Men, of course, are by no means excluded from this investigation of the hair. Some years ago, it was considered decidedly effeminate for men to have anything other than a

'short back and sides' cut. Now they have as wide a choice
as women. In addition, there is the question of whether or
not to grow a beard and/or moustache. Why not experiment in this direction? The right sort of beard, if kept
neatly trimmed, can be a real asset for some men, and will
certainly change the appearance.

The main objective, for both men and women, is to find
a style that will suit their personality, is comfortable, and
will feel right for them. If you have worn your hair in the
same way for more years than you care to remember and,
after trying other styles, still prefer the original one, then
by all means return to it. But do try other possibilities first.

Naturally, it goes without saying, that it is essential for
hair to be clean and tidy, whatever the style. When we are
ill and unable to wash our hair for a while, it is amazing
how much better we feel once we can do this again.

Consider, then, the state of your hair by a careful
examination in those mirrors, and then act accordingly.

3. CLOTHES

We now turn to the question of clothes; another important
aspect, and again, these will tell us a great deal about their
wearer. Those going for a job interview will, if they are
wise, give careful forethought to how they will dress for
the event. It is most important to give the correct impres-
sion to a prospective employer. Smart clothes do not have
to be expensive or new, but they must be spotlessly clean,
well pressed and, as with the hair style, they must be
appropriate to the age and temperament of the person
wearing them.

Look critically at the clothes you are wearing now.
Could you, without necessarily buying new ones, improve
on your appearance? Whatever we wear, we should feel
relaxed and comfortable in it, and know that it is helping
to give the image we wish to convey.

Some points to aim for would be:

a. Think about colour matching. For a woman it is usually
   best to have a single basic colour for accessories like

shoes, bag, belt, etc. The colour of a man's tie should tone with his suit and shirt, or if he is wearing casual clothes, the combination of colours should look right. It is easy enough, nowadays, to buy colour-co-ordinated clothes in the large stores.

b. Keep clothes pressed and brushed. Hang them carefully in the wardrobe when not in use. This will not only ensure that they maintain their fresh appearance, but will give them a longer lease of life.

c. Try to wear something different each day. This will not necessitate a very extensive wardrobe; merely that you ring the changes in order to give yourself variety. It may only be a change of brooch, blouse or collar or, for a man, a different tie, or socks or colour of shirt. You might try wearing a button-hole, especially if you have a garden and so easy access to an assortment of flowers.

d. If you need to buy new clothes, resolve to be a little adventurous.

If you have always been conservative in your tastes, don't attempt to be outrageously so, but look around for something that is just marginally different from anything you have worn before. You may be surprised at the pleasure it will bring you. Should you feel that this would be embarrassing, you could experiment, instead, on a new type of underwear; anything that will give you a slightly different image.

4. HEALTH

Having considered posture, hair, and clothes we will now move on to the question of health. Many people who live alone give too little thought to this important subject. Food, in particular, can receive little attention. Whilst not going short of food, we can very easily make do with a low standard of nourishment, either from trying to economise, or because we choose meals that will take the least possible trouble to prepare. So-called 'junk food', quickly prepared snacks, and ready-made 'take-aways' seldom provide a balanced diet. We need to remember that it is not necessary to cook elaborate meals, or spend a long time in their preparation. Cold dishes and raw ingredients often contain as many essential vitamins and proteins (and sometimes more) than an oven-cooked meal. If we have an inadequate diet we will soon find ourselves in poor health; tired, listless, and prone to pick up any virus that may be around.

Never skip meals, and try to eat at regular intervals, making sure that your daily consumption will include some protein foods (choose from cheese, eggs, fish, meat or nuts), fresh fruit and vegetables, and wholemeal cereals or bread. Milk and other dairy produce is good, but if you are watching your figure, opt for skimmed rather than full-cream milk. Too much fat and sugar should be avoided, and although tea and coffee can be drunk in moderation, it is better not to have too much caffeine, so an occasional glass of fruit juice would make a healthier alternative.

Check again in the mirror, this time to see if you are over-weight. If you are, this will inevitably prevent your feeling or looking your best, so you must do something about it. Many lonely people will 'eat for comfort', and be almost unaware that they are doing so. Little nibbles throughout the day seem harmless enough, but it is these that do the damage. If you want to reduce your weight, here are the rules to observe:

a. Reduce the amount of fat and sugar you eat each day. Do this by having skimmed milk and fat-reduced cheese, cutting all fat off meat (before, not after, cooking), using sweeteners instead of sugar and, if you have tinned fruit, choosing that in natural juice rather than syrup. If you like museli, buy the sugar-free type, and sweeten it by adding a few sultanas or a sliced banana. Try to avoid fried food.

b. DON'T cut out your sweet treats entirely if you enjoy these, but reduce the number you eat. Ration yourself to no more than one chocolate bar a day, or one cake, but not both. Buy no more biscuits as these are very full of calories, and the same applies to sweets. The trouble with sweets is that it is hard to limit yourself to one only; much easier to cut them out altogether.

c. Never allow yourself to eat between meals. It's those little tit-bits that put on the pounds.

d. Apart from the items already suggested, continue to eat the foods you enjoy. BUT, cut down the size of your portions and don't allow yourself second helpings. Serve your main meal on a smaller plate. It will look more!

e. Bread is not too fattening, but what you put on it usually is, so limit yourself to no more than two slices per meal.

f. It is better to have four, or even five SMALL meals per day that two large ones. You will then have something nice to which you can look forward, without too long an interval between.

g. Make sure that, as you are eating less food, what you do have contains the maximum nourishment.

h. Cut down on alcohol. It very quickly increases your weight.

By observing these rules you will lose weight slowly, and this is the best way to do it. Never be tempted to go on a starvation or 'crash' diet. While this method will appear to be very effective at first, your weight will rise again as soon as you come off it. In fact, it is likely to go up even more. This is because our bodies respond to a 'famine situation' by storing up extra fat, and will convert the food we eat into a reserve of fat, instead of using it to provide energy.

Personal freshness

When I was young, deodorants had just come on to the market, and advertisements rather coyly hinted that we might be unaware of a personal problem which even friends would hesitate to mention. It is, however, quite true that others may be more conscious of the unpleasant odour of stale perspiration than we ourselves, so that it is important to use a deodorant daily. We should also not forget that the excessive application of strong perfume may be almost equally repellent, for a pleasing scent to one person may be quite repulsive to another. A man, too, may find others recoiling from his over-enthusiastic use of an after-shave. Discretion and moderation is usually the best policy.

Smoking

As a child, I grew up in an atmosphere thick with smoke, for my mother enjoyed cigarettes and my father a pipe. At Christmas, he would indulge in a cigar or two, so that the smell of cigar smoke holds happy memories for me. It was, in those days, thought to be most unsociable not to offer friends a cigarette when they called, and non-smokers would keep a supply in the house for the benefit of visitors. Today, the reverse is true, and smokers are not always appreciated, particularly in restaurants or other enclosed places where people gather. In addition to this, we are warned emphatically by doctors that smoking can damage our health. for these reasons, if you feel able, it is advisable to cut down your smoking, or to stop it altogether. This will be up to you, and, because you are already having to make a great many changes in your life, you may not be able to achieve it. Don't worry if you can't. But if you are able to do so it will be a feather in your cap, and an added bonus.

Warmth

In the winter it is vital to have sufficient heating in your home. Hypothermia is a hazard, particularly for the elderly living alone. If you find it difficult to meet the cost of fuel bills, do check to see if you are eligible for a heating allowance from the Social Security. Gas and electricity companies will try to help older people by spreading the cost of payments throughout the year, and will not cut off supplies in the depths of winter if you are having problems and explain your circumstances to them. It may help to heat just one room in the house, living and sleeping there temporarily in a severe winter. Hot water bottles are good friends, and older people can make themselves really cosy with the help of shawls and blankets. Wrap up well in several layers of woollen clothing. Nourishing food, too, helps us to stay warm, so stoke up with piping hot soups and stews in really cold weather. Remember, though, that the best and healthiest warmer of all is exercise, so, unless you are very elderly or infirm, a brisk daily walk is your first priority.

Regular dental and eye checks

These are essential for good health, and you must not neglect them. Many eye defects, which can cause damage to sight and even blindness, are easily corrected if they are detected in the early stages. The misery of painful toothache and loss of teeth can be avoided by dental check-ups. If it is a considerable time since you last visited your optician or dentist, it will be in your own interest to put this right before leaving *ROOM 3*.

5. CHRISTMAS

Christmas can be a particularly difficult time for those living alone, so these guidelines may help to make it more enjoyable:

1. Begin well before Christmas to prepare as for a siege. Build up a store of your favourite foods. Plan a small treat for every meal throughout the holiday period. Include drinks, chocolates, and other luxuries, even if you don't normally indulge in them. Diets can be suspended for a day or so. Spoil yourself! Buy books and puzzles and put them away until the holiday. Think of a new hobby you could start then. Make a list of letters to write. Don't forget games which can be played alone like patience, scrabble or crosswords. Try to make up a crossword puzzle yourself. This is not as hard as it sounds. You can copy the 'grid' pattern from a newspaper, and then fit in words, working out the clues last. Many magazines or local

papers will pay for puzzles sent in, so you might even earn yourself a little money.

2. Warmth. This is essential. Be sure to have a warm and comfortable house or, at least, one really warm room. Don't try to economise.

3. Buy the T.V. Times. Plan the programmes you would like most to watch or hear.

4. Make out a detailed and varied programme for each day. Aim to go out for a short time every day, if the weather permits. A brisk walk, even when the shops are closed, will give you an appetite for those extra special meals.

5. Treat yourself to a visit to a pantomime, play, film, concert, or even a school Christmas show.

6. On Christmas Day, put on your best clothes to mark the occasion. It doesn't matter that you are alone and no-one else will see. It will make YOU feel better.

7. Go to a church service, or watch one on television. This, after all, is what Christmas is all about, and the familiar carols will lift your spirits.

8. During the holiday, try to help someone less fortunate than yourself. Find out if there are old people in a hospital or a home who would appreciate a visit. Ask the Social Services or your local church where help is needed.

9. Finally, don't expect people to come and visit you and then feel aggrieved when they don't. Make up your mind that you will be on your own and ENJOY it.

Do not suppose that you have, all this while, escaped the notice of that lurking gremlin. He will be having plenty to say to you, so be ready for such discouraging remarks as these:

Gremlin: "You can't possibly cope with all these tedious chores. It won't matter if you skip a few."
ANSWER: It will matter very much. You are aiming in this Room to make the very best of your personality, and

nothing less will do.

Gremlin: "Most of this doesn't apply to you, anyway. You are all right as you are."

ANSWER: There is always room for some improvement. The mirrors in the room are here to show you where change is needed. They, not the gremlin, are your true guides.

Gremlin: "You are too old to bother with all this."

ANSWER: No-one is too old. Why should age matter? Throughout the whole of our lives self-esteem is always worth preserving.

Gremlin: "Thinking of yourself is nothing but conceit."

ANSWER: This is untrue. We have a responsibility, not only to ourselves but to others, to appear at our best. Taking proper care of our bodies is only sensible, and is a sure way of improving health and happiness.

To study all these aspects of self-care, and to work on improving your own image, is going to take some time, and you will have to be prepared to linger in this room for quite a while before tackling the next stage of your journey. Do not continue until you are satisfied that you are doing all that is in your power to make the most of yourself.

Take a final check in those mirrors, and then you will be able to go forward with confidence. Ahead of you now is Door 4, and on it the notice, '*CURRENT AFFAIRS*'.

The Fourth Door – Current Affairs

You are hesitating, perhaps, as you look at this door. Surely it is not necessary to go through THIS room. It is, I'm afraid. There is no short cut here, and the only way forward is to go straight on. Don't worry. It will not be nearly as difficult as you suppose. In fact, you are probably going to enjoy it.

Open that door and take a glance into the room. It is a warm and comfortable place, with papers, magazines and books strewn around, a fireside chair, and a television and radio conveniently placed. It appears to be quite welcoming, so go up to the table and have a look at what is there. First of all, you will find a pile of newspapers; all the national dailies and weeklies and, in a separate heap, those produced by the local Press for your area.

Go through all the daily papers and compare them. You will notice that they differ from each other quite considerably. The tabloids concentrate mainly on stories about personalities, which will catch our attention. The larger papers, the big national papers, will be first reporting on international news, and the stories of human interest, though still accorded a place, will have less coverage. If you read every paper carefully, you will be able to detect in most of them a bias towards one particular political party, so that while one is praising some move by the Government, another will criticise it.

Which daily paper do you read, and why did you choose it? Perhaps its cheerful gossipy stories, its cartoon strips, details of the day's television and radio programmes, the crossword puzzle, or its sports pages have the most appeal for you. Most papers include these, and there is no reason at all why you should not enjoy them. However, this room is concerned with the more serious aspects of world affairs, so it is these features at which we shall be mainly looking. You will now have a daily assignment of carefully reading through all the political news which your paper reports. This will include all that is currently happening in countries abroad, as well as events in Parliament here. For those of you who have been accustomed in the past to skip these pages, it may seem a dull and formidable task, but you will find it well worth while. To keep abreast of current affairs will help you to join intelligently in conversation with others, and to have a far better understanding of the world around you. As you read of global events, check in the atlas from *ROOM 1* that you are quite sure where these are taking place. In addition to carefully reading your newspaper, you must also watch at least one television news bulletin daily, or listen to its equivalent on the radio. If you have poor sight, and so are excused from reading the newspaper, it is even more important to use your radio to learn about world news.

Current affairs programmes on television are not most people's first choice, and with other channels from which to select, it is easy enough to avoid them altogether. You must now resolve to watch at least one every week, so find something which will not clash with your favourite soap opera or sports event, and view it regularly. You may well find it boring at first, but remember how you discovered in *ROOM 1* that a subject can become much more interesting as we learn more about it.

When an election is near, short Party Political broadcasts are made at frequent intervals. They are usually shown simultaneously on both main channels, in order to ensure the largest possible audience. Despite this, it is more than likely that many people will either sigh and switch off when one is announced, or use that ten minutes or so to wash the dishes, or put the baby to bed. Nevertheless, these broadcasts have their value, and you should try to watch them. They are, of course, intentional propaganda for the various parties, stressing the good each has achieved and ignoring any failures, but if you watch them all, you will be able to weigh one against the other and decide which is best.

We all have a responsibility to support a parliamentary party, and to give our vote to the candidate representing it at General Elections. We should know why we consider one party preferable to another, and not be guilty of just picking a name at random, or even worse, not bothering to vote at all. We tend to take for granted our privilege to have an elected government, and because we have not lived in a country where people have no freedom of choice, we may not realise how fortunate we are. Being at liberty to live our lives as we wish is a very precious thing. During the last war many temporary restrictions were imposed and were extremely irksome. I can still remember the frustration I felt at being unable to change from office work to teaching until hostilities were over, because of a law which prohibited a move from one occupation to another.

You may already be quite certain in your own mind which political party you prefer. Once you are sure of this, have another look at your daily newspaper to see if it also reflects your views. Perhaps you will find some papers easier to read than others, and now may be the time to switch to a different one. Be careful in your choice. It is quite a good idea, when you are reading the political news, to keep a little notebook and jot down the names of the various prime ministers in other countries, or those holding important positions in our own government. If nothing else, think how gratifying it will be if, because of gaining this extra knowledge, you find yourself knowing all the answers on a quiz programme.

It really is important to be certain which political party you support and why you do so. Sometimes, a television reporter will take a microphone into the streets, and ask people, at random, their opinion on some current topic. So often he will simply get a blank look, or a mumbled 'Don't know'. There are, in our time, a great many controversial issues, about which we should certainly hold some definite views of our own. Are you, for example, against or in favour of abortion, capital punishment, the Sunday opening of shops, or women priests? Are modern teaching methods adequate? Is our society too permissive? Could there be fairer methods of taxation? What can be done about football hooliganism?

These are all questions of national interest, and are covered by the daily papers, but we must not forget about local affairs. Some of these could be of considerable importance and relevance to you. In many towns old people find themselves at risk, because of uneven pavements, dangerous traffic conditions, or roads in a state of bad repair. Poorly-lit streets may be a hazard, or perhaps there are long waiting lists for hospital treatment, an inadequate bus service, or areas made unsightly by an accumulation of litter. These matters are dealt with by the Urban or Rural District Council and, if we are dissatisfied with conditions in the area, this is the authority responsible. It is in our own interests to be aware of events and amenities in our own neighbourhood, and activities at this level will be covered by the local Press. Most areas have free weekly sheets giving such information, so it is always readily available.

If you have a complaint, comment, or word of praise for something that has taken place in your particular town or village, the editor of your local paper will usually welcome a letter about it, and will often publish these in his columns. It is good for us not only to take an interest, but to become involved in neighbourhood affairs. Be sure, then, to read your local paper, and be on the look out for meetings, talks, sales, or social events that you might be able to attend.

When elections take place, whether a general election for the whole Government, a by-election for the M.P. for your area only, or a local council election, be sure to record your vote. Think carefully about it, for although a single vote may seem of little worth, each counts towards the whole and will influence the result.

Although we are all, to some extent, affected by them, not everyone takes an equal interest in current affairs. You will not, therefore, be expected to do more than the following, once you have left this room. This much, however, will be required of you:

1. To select carefully your daily newspaper.
2. To regularly read both it and the local news, paying particular attention to political events.
3. To watch at least one current affairs programme on the television each week, or listen to one on the radio.
4. To determine which political party you support, and always make use of your vote at elections.

For those of you who find politics fascinating, though, further steps may be taken, but these are optional. You may consider writing to your M.P., offering support to the party by helping at elections, displaying posters, addressing envelopes, etc. There will be political meetings and talks to attend. In addition to this, there are sometimes local ratepayers associations or neighbourhood watch schemes where new members would be welcomed, so if these activities would interest you, by all means find out more about them. Lectures or classes on current affairs may be available in your area. If you are really keen, you could even aspire to become a local councillor yourself.

The gremlin of *ROOM 4* has been waiting impatiently for his turn to speak.

Gremlin: "This is a thoroughly boring subject, and you are not in the least interested. Why not skip it?"

ANSWER: To continue the journey, it is obligatory to go through this room. Some duties ARE dull, but they are necessary, and the knowledge gained here will be very valuable.

Gremlin: "You already have quite enough to do each day. There is no time to read all that tedious political news."

ANSWER: It is true that most of your spare time is being taken up, but your intention is to live a full and varied life.

It may not be possible to carry out the tasks and assignments of every room daily; some can be done on alternative days, or once a week. However, the newspapers MUST be read daily, and preferably at a set time allocated for this to suit your own convenience.

Gremlin: "The subject of politics only causes arguments and should be avoided in conversations, so why waste time on it?"

ANSWER: Having political opinions does not mean that we have to force them on our fellows. It is usually those with only limited knowledge who are dogmatic about it, and refuse to listen to others. Informed discussion on current affairs can make for very interesting conversation.

When you have silenced the gremlin and worked out your programme for using this room, you may proceed to *ROOM 5*. Here you will find a completely different subject, for the label on the door is '*CREATIVITY*'.

The Fifth Door – Creativity

You will notice, as you open this door, that the room is quite different from those through which you have already passed. It is small, circular, and quite empty, except for a table in the centre, where you will find various numbered boxes filled with cards. All round the walls are little doors, each numbered, and leading into an even smaller room. You will need to go through only one of these. The choice, and it is a very wide one, will be entirely up to you.

Have a closer look at the boxes. The cards they contain describe various activities you may wish to undertake, and each box covers a different type of skill. You may feel that you are not a creative sort of person, that your fingers are all thumbs, and you are hopeless at every variety of art and craft. Don't worry. Creativity can be expressed in so many ways, and you are sure to find something here that you can do, or learn to do.

You will be free to select either an occupation you are familiar with already, or perhaps decide to embark on an entirely new one. The range will cover skills of hand, mind or body, practical or artistic work, making collections of all kinds, specialised hobbies or sports, or, indeed, any undertaking that you really enjoy for its own sake. The purpose of this room is to give you both pleasure and the satisfaction of achievement, and your aim will be either to discover a new field of interest, or to improve on a skill you already possess.

You will not feel yourself under pressure in this room. There is no daily assignment. You simply have to choose a subject with which to occupy yourself; something which you will enjoy doing. The amount of time you spend on it is for you to decide, and you will be able to fit it into odd moments of the day, or to devote longer periods to it as you feel inclined. You will be doing it for relaxation rather than as a duty.

The time has come for you to select your card, so we will look at the boxes in turn. Each contains a set of cards corresponding to the category with which the box is labelled.

BOX 1. NEEDLECRAFT

Although generally considered to be of interest only to women, this need not necessarily be so. I have a set of beautifully embroidered pictures made by a man, and many of our leading clothes and knitwear designers are men.

a. *Needlework.* This will include the making of clothes or household linen, embroidery with wool or silk, patchwork, felt craft and so on.

b. *Knitting or crochet.* If you already know the basic stitches, now is the time to attempt more advanced work, and perhaps learn to use a knitting machine.

c. *Soft toys.* These are much in demand at sales, and there is a wide range of patterns available. Safety eyes must always be used to conform to legal requirements.

d. *Dress or hat designing.* Plenty of skill is required here, and there is scope for originality, if this is your interest.

e. *Spinning and weaving.* You may like to learn how to use a spinning wheel or loom; a very ancient craft.

f. *Jewellery making.* Ear-rings, using beads and wire, are quite easy to make, and there are many other ways of threading beads and making attractive ornaments with a variety of materials.

BOX 2. HANDICRAFTS

While *BOX 1* would appeal mostly to women, the cards in *BOX 2* will mainly be chosen by men but, again, it is a matter for personal preference.

a. Wood carving.

b. Metal work.

c. Glass engraving.

d. Picture framing.

e. Pottery.

f. Upholstery.

g. Model or toy making.

BOX 3. D.I.Y. OR PRACTICAL WORK

a. House decorating, painting, paperhanging.

b. Furniture making or renovation.

BOX 4. SPECIAL INTEREST ACTIVITIES

a. Painting: In oils or in water colours.

b. Brass rubbing.

c. Photography.

d. Drama: This would include taking part in amateur dramatics, stage management, or helping with props and lighting.

e. Flower arranging or pressed flower work.

f. Cookery: This has many possibilities from the most basic skills to Cordon Bleu.

g. Bee keeping: A profitable as well as fascinating hobby.

h. Fishing.

i. Learning to play a musical instrument or to sing in a choir.

j. The study of wild flowers and their folk lore.

k. Bird watching.

l. Train spotting or steam railway preservation.

BOX 5. USING MACHINES

a. Typewriters, manual or electric.

b. Word processors.

c. Computers.

BOX 6. PHYSICAL SKILLS

a. Dancing. This could include Morris, Old Tyme, Country (English, Scottish, Irish or American Square Dancing), or Modern.

b. Horse riding or pony treking.

c. Fencing.

d. Judo.

e. Gymnastics or Aerobics.

f. Hang gliding.

g. Wind surfing.

h. Skating (ice or roller skates).

i. Body building or weight lifting.

BOX 7. MENTAL SKILLS

a. Learning to play bridge, chess or scrabble.

b. Learning another language.

c. Learning to write articles, stories or poetry.

d. Learning more about literature or poetry at a special class or literary circle.

BOX 8. MAKING COLLECTIONS

a. Antiques.

b. Postage stamps.

c. Scrapbooks (collections of cuttings of anything, or objects of interest that can be pasted into a book).

d. Coins.

e. Small interesting objects or souvenirs (e.g. thimbles, teddy bears).

If you have a special interest which has not been catered for here, (perhaps you are a jig-saw devotee, a cross-word puzzle addict, or have a desire to research your family tree), it is permissible to make out a card for this yourself, and add it to those in the appropriate box. Once you have chosen your card, or more than one if you are really keen and have the time to spare, then you must take it to the small room which has been allocated to your particular skill. The number on the door will match that on your card. Here will be instructions to help you. For the most part, you will be directed to your local library for reference books, or to your educational authority for details of classes in the subject you have chosen.

If you have decided to tackle something entirely new, don't feel apprehensive. You are not expected to be an expert when you first start, but everyone improves with practice. We have to fall off several times before we can ride a bicycle without wobbling, and this applies to all other skills. Just make a start, and before long you will find yourself enjoying it.

Because the activities here are pleasurable and ones in which you have an interest, you will seldom have any trouble from a gremlin. They will all be congregating in rooms further ahead, where they hope to have a better chance of disrupting your progress. So, while you are here, make the most of it. You have worked hard and deserve some relaxation. You have reached an easier stage of the journey, for when you are ready to try the next room, you will find that it is labelled 'RECREATION'.

The Sixth Door – Recreation

The time has come for you to enjoy a break in what you are probably finding quite an arduous journey. Door 6 will open, not into a room, as have the others, but into a narrow side passage, leading through an archway and out into the open air. Here, for a while, you can forget about duties and obligations, and simply feel free to relax and be yourself.

It is fitting that after having been concerned with creativity, you should now have the opportunity to re-create your own energies. This is an elementary principle of life. The day's toil must be followed by the night's rest; summer's growth by winter's sleep. No employer can expect good service from his staff, unless he provides them with breaks in the working day. Children at school enjoy their morning, lunch-time and afternoon playtime periods, and students are advised that they will become stale and unfit to cope with an examination paper, if they sit up all the previous night revising their work. It is very true that 'All work and no play, makes Jack a dull boy'.

If we try to take too much out of a battery, we only find that it becomes progressively weaker and lets us down. This necessary re-charging with power applies in the same way to humans. We get more done in a day if we allow ourselves short breaks for relaxation, than if we try to carry on without interruption. Variety, too, will make work easier, because prolonged hours spent on a monotonous task lead to exhaustion. Meal times should be long enough to include time for relaxation. It is a mistake to snatch a hasty sandwich while continuing to work. Ideally, we should set aside at least half an hour for resting after every meal, before continuing with the day's tasks. It is not good to leap up and wash the dishes immediately after swallowing the last mouthful of food.

Pressures of modern working life frequently cause stress which, in excess, can be responsible for much ill-health. This stress can be reduced by regular periods of relaxation. Before the days of television, many people would treat themselves to a weekly visit to the cinema, followed, perhaps, by tea in the cinema cafe. This made for a very pleasant afternoon, and was an occasion which could be anticipated with pleasure. It was customary, also, to go for leisurely family walks, or to have musical evenings around the piano. Nowadays, of course, we relax when work is done in front of the television, which is certainly pleasant, but probably not so beneficial, because it is there all the time and so soon take for granted.

Sport will be catered for in a room further along the route, so we will consider pastimes apart from this. You will be aiming now to slow yourself down, in order to renew your energies for the rest of the journey, so you must look for some sort of recreation which you will really enjoy. It may be gardening, rambling, or if you have a car, taking a little run in the country. You might even try a day or a half-day coach excusion. There are board or card games, listening to music, doing crossword or similar puzzles, and countless other possibilities.

It is quite permissible to take a day off, now and again, from the assignments you have already been given. For older people it is often helpful to allow yourself to have a little sleep during the day; a short afternoon nap is refreshing, but should not be for too long in duration, or you may have trouble in sleeping at night. A rocking-chair is very soothing for the nerves, and the comfort and company of a pet can also assist you to unwind after the tensions of the day. Many people also find it relaxing to chat to a friend on the telephone.

In previous rooms you have often been referred to

books as a means of obtaining information and further knowledge. Reading has additional uses and is a wonderful means of escape. Whether you plunge into the worlds of science fiction, romance, detection, days of old, or high adventure, you can, for a while at least, forget present troubles and pressures, and lose yourself in a make-believe environment. This is beneficial, and can certainly be recommended as an aid to restful sleep, if you set aside half an hour or so with a book at the end of the day. It is never wise to work right up to the time of going to bed. Winding down is important.

Never feel that time spent in recreation is time wasted. It is quite the reverse, and is an essential ingredient for good health. It is very refreshing to allow your mind to rest, day dream and to lie fallow for a while. "What is this life," said W.H. Davies, "if full of care, we have no time to stand and stare?" And he was quite right in seeing the value of this.

Do not neglect your recreation time. It is your means of building up the strength you are going to need for difficult areas of that part of the journey still lying ahead. Wait until you are sure that you feel really rested and refreshed. Once this has been achieved, you must then look for your passport. You have not studied this for some time, but you will need it now. Before re-entering the corridor and continuing on your way to *ROOM 7*, it must be shown at the turnstile through which you have to pass.

Take the opportunity of reading it through again, and reminding yourself of the resolutions you have made. There may be tough assignments still to be undertaken. Take heart, though. You have already achieved a great deal, and nothing impossible or beyond your capabilities is going to be required of you. After presenting the passport, you will find yourself once more in the main corridor with the door of *ROOM 7* ahead. It is a large and heavy door, and on it you will see an impressive title: '*SCIENCE, RELIGION AND PHILOSOPHY*'.

The Seventh Door – Science, Religion and Philosophy

This is a vast room, much larger than any you have yet entered. As you open the door, you will see that it extends far into the distance, and that it contains many separate compartments, each well stocked with books and papers. Machines, some looking very complicated, fill shelves and benches, and there is a great deal of scientific equipment to be seen. Do not be over-awed, however, at such a display, nor by the complexity of the subjects you will be contemplating here. There is abundant choice available, and you are only going to study, at your own level, that which interests you, and which you will find useful and of relevance in your own daily life.

You may be puzzled that three subjects are included, each apparently very different from the others. Actually they are closely related, for the purpose of all three is to find some meaning and purpose in life; to discover the great truths behind this mysterious universe in which we find ourselves.

You may feel that this should be left to scholars and scientists, and is of little concern to you. Perhaps you think that it is all too difficult for the ordinary man or woman in the street. Nothing could be further from the truth. We all possess brains, and they are meant to be used. It is most important for us to think about life, and work out our own conclusions about it. They may not be correct, but they will satisfy us and give our living some purpose. Those who choose a blinkered existence, uncaring of all that goes on around them, will soon become bored and discontented. They will certainly be lonely; locked into their own limited and self-centred world.

Let us, then, have a look at the three ways in which, while we are in this room, we shall be thinking about life and its meaning.

SCIENCE

All through history, men have tried to discover why the world is as it is. Primitive peoples feared thunder and earthquakes, volcanos and hurricanes, without understanding them. They believed that the world was flat, so that if you were foolish enough to venture too close to the horizon, you would plunge over the edge into a bottomless abyss. They thought that the sun travelled round the earth, and that the earth itself was the centre of the universe. They gazed in awe at the rainbow and the starry skies. But gradually knowledge increased, as they learned by trial and error to comprehend the fundamental laws of nature. In these days we have learned to take for granted the power of electricity, gas and nuclear fission, and to harness them for our use. No doubt, in centuries to come, new and equally miraculous discoveries will be made.

What, though, has all this to do with us in the twentieth century? A very great deal. Life has changed tremendously in recent years, and we need to understand a little, at least, about modern technology if we are to enjoy the benefits of television, central heating, microwave ovens, washing machines and so on, even if we have no wish to drive a car or work a computer. Also, recent research has been making us aware of possible damage to the environment by the use of particular chemical products, and this is something that should surely concern us.

Science itself, as a subject to be studied at school or college, will interest some people more than others. Elementary science; for example, learning about magnets, the way light can be split into its rainbow colours, the formation of crystals, etc., is very interesting, and not hard to understand, but at a higher level, we do need to have an aptitude for and understanding of mathematics. Another branch of science is a study of the stars, and this, again, can be undertaken at a very simple level; just learning about the planets in our own solar system, and being able to locate the well-known constellations, such as the Plough, in the night sky.

Personally, I have always found science a difficult subject. I once picked up a text book belonging to my niece, when she was at university, and found that, although I understood up to about half-way down the first page, the remaining contents of the book were completely incomprehensible to me, and might just as well have been written in Arabic!

So don't worry! You are not going to be asked to study at that level. All you need to do is to find out a little more about the world around you. If your present understanding of scientific matters is strictly limited, your best plan will be, as in *ROOM 1*, to consult the children's section of the library for books about the stars, electricity, light, air and water, gravity etc. Ladybird Books do a very good informative series. Of course, if the subject interests you, and you are already reasonably well informed, you can go much deeper. Space travel, for instance, is a fascinating subject.

PHILOSOPHY AND RELIGION

Although these subjects differ widely in many ways, we can, for convenience, consider them together.

Science searches for truth by using reason and logic. Nothing is accepted unless it has been proved beyond all doubt. However, there is much in life that cannot be tied down in this way, and yet obviously exists. These truths we discover by intuition and feeling. Philosophy and religion are concerned with exploring qualities of beauty, truth and goodness, which are not only found in the world of nature, but can be expressed by mankind through music, poetry and art. To understand life more fully, we have to use both brain and heart; our intellect and reasoning certainly, but also our minds, instincts and feelings.

Early man, puzzled by the mystery of how the world came into being and the purpose of it, began to form theories which became woven into myth and legend, each race developing its own. The question of how the earth remained in the sky perplexed many, one idea being that it was carried on the back of a huge turtle; another, that it was supported in the heavens on the shoulders of the giant Atlas. Men began to understand that mere chance could not account for the wonders of the earth around them, and it was supposed that supernatural beings, gods, goddesses, or spirits must be responsible.

For many centuries, however, the time of primitive man was fully occupied in searching for food and shelter, and the need to protect himself from wild beasts. Tribe fought with tribe in order to maintain the territories necessary for their very existence. Eventually, though, as civilization grew, men realised that they had needs beyond mere animal survival. They longed to understand and find purpose in life; they sought happiness and fulfilment. Ideals of unselfishness, courage, generosity, kindness and love were seen to be worthy, while evil was recognised as being opposed to good. These values were woven into the mythological stories of the race, and passed down from one generation to another.

Myths are not merely stories. They reveal elements of truth, and the search for understanding. Out of them grew religious thought, as men tried to form ideas of the nature of a God they instinctively felt the need to worship.

The religions of the world as we know it today differ a great deal from each other, in doctrine and practice, yet still have much in common; essentially that basic urge to discover a relationship with God. Their differences, however, have led to bitter wars, rivalry, persecution and hatred over many centuries. It is probably good that, in our time, the mingling of different races within a country has helped us to have a somewhat better understanding of religions and cultures other than our own.

Philosophical thought does not necessarily attach itself to any one religion, or indeed to religion at all. There are many humanists and atheists, for example, who do not consider that they have to explain life in terms of a deity in any form.

Your purpose in this room, then, is to look at some of the material available to you here. You can examine the many different creeds and beliefs and then form your own opinion. It is entirely for you to decide. The important thing is to have views of your own on human life and its purpose. To assist you, the room is designed to allow you to browse through all the resources that will help you to make up your mind. There is no hurry and your task should be a pleasant one. Enjoy reading again simple versions of the Greek, Roman, Norse, North American Indian, Egyptian, Hindu, Japanese and Chinese myths. Again, if they are quite unknown to you, I would recommend your finding them first in children's literature. Enquire at your library. I was, myself, particularly fascinated by the Norse myths when I discovered them.

Then, if you have some interest in a particular religion and would like to know more about it, find books on this, or enquire at the church in question. Even if you already attend a church, do think about your faith to check that you are really sure of all your beliefs. We should never accept a faith because we are taught it parrot-fashion by parents or teachers. To be real and worthwhile it must be personal to us. Do not be afraid to question belief, and if you are puzzled or doubtful, find someone who is qualified to guide and help you. There is only one truth, and that is the only thing worth seeking. There are, inevitably, some questions that we cannot answer with any certainty, but we should still face them and think about them.

Small children will often ask us very penetrating questions which, perhaps, as adults, we have simply shelved. A five-year-old asked me "Who made God?", and most of us at some time have wondered why there is so much pain and suffering in the world, or what we shall find on the other side of death. We need to consider these things, and in this room there will be an opportunity to do so.

You may be quite certain that at, or before this point, your will will be barred by at least one gremlin. *ROOM 7* is a favourite spot for them to gather in order to pour scorn on something that is, in their opinion, extremely difficult and requiring serious thought. They fully expect some travellers to find these subjects too much for them, and that they can now be persuaded to give up their quest.

Gremlin: "All this is way above your head and much too difficult for you."

ANSWER: Not at all. It can be studied at a very elementary level, and only those aspects which already hold some interest and appeal need be followed up.

Gremlin: "You are studying many different subjects now, so surely you can do without all this serious stuff."

ANSWER: That is true for people who are content to be ill-informed cabbages, or feather-brains with no sensible thoughts in their heads.

Gremlin: "What has scientific and religious mumbo-jumbo to do with whether or not you are going to be lonely?"

ANSWER: Quite a lot. We cannot hold interesting conversations with others if we have no opinions of our own.

It is worthwhile lingering in *ROOM 7*, because there is much to discover here and, as well as exploring libraries and bookshops for new knowledge, there are other places well worth a visit. If you live near London, the Science Museum, for example, should not be missed. Museums are no longer dull exhibitions of boring objects in glass cases. The Science Museum, in particular, offers displays, working models, slides and well set up and entertaining features of all kinds. Another completely different, but equally intriguing place is the London Planetarium, which can be commended to anyone wishing to know more about astronomy.

When you are satisfied that you have made a start on the ground you would like to cover, and have decided how much time you can devote to it, you will be ready for the next stage of the journey. You will find quite a contrast in the room that follows on from this for, as you approach the door, you will see that it is labelled '*HUMOUR*'.

The Eighth Door – Humour

It has been said that a sense of humour is one of Man's greatest assets, and to be able to 'see the funny side of things' will greatly ease our journey through life. The same is true of this journey out of loneliness. We must learn to laugh, and especially to be able to laugh at ourselves. It is a mistake to view life too solemnly, for we are capable of many moods, and one of these is mirth.

It was necessary to spend time in serious thought in the previous room. Here, though, in contrast, you will be able to relax again. You will find *ROOM 8* a pleasant place, and you need have no apprehension about opening the door and exploring its possibilities.

You will find yourself in a small, bright room, with many open windows, each revealing a restful view of lawns, trees and flowers. Here you will find that humour will help to offset any weariness brought about by your long journey.

First, though, you will need to think carefully about the nature of humour, for if it is forced and artificial, it is worthless. You will, perhaps, remember Mona Lot in Tommy Handley's sketches, a caricature of the person who goes through life in a perpetual state of discontentment, and sums up every situation with, 'Isn't it terrible!'. There are those who, in an attempt to avoid this attitude to life, will adopt a bright and breezy manner wherever they go, clapping others on the back and trying to be the life and soul of every party. Needless to say, they are seldom popular. Even worse are those who think themselves great comedians, and force others to listen to their ancient and, more often than not, feeble jokes. You have probably encountered the self-styled wit, who will pin you into a corner while he recites a tedious 'shaggy dog' story, the punch line of which he has either forgotten or misinterpreted. The practical joker, who enjoys the discomfiture of others, has no place here either. None of this is genuine humour.

If you can develop a cheerful manner; to greet others at all times with a smile and an encouraging word, to make light of small mishaps, and not be afraid to laugh when you yourself make foolish mistakes, you will be well on the way to discovering it.

"A merry heart goes all the way
Your sad tyres in a mire are" runs the old song, and, as Gracie Fields used to tell us, "A song and smile makes your life worth while".

It is all too easy to fall into the habit of complaining and seeing the negative side of everything. When people ask how we are, it is so tempting to real off detailed catalogues of woes and ailments, which make depressing listening for the long-suffering friend or acquaintance who has enquired. It is far better to make light of them, saving the gory details for the doctor's ear. He is, after all, paid to listen and possibly to alleviate them. Concentrating on grievances, pains and misfortunes does nothing to lessen them. Helen Keller, who from a very early age was both blind and deaf, and so had more reason than most to feel that life had treated her badly, said that the one thing she had learned was that you must "never, never, NEVER, feel sorry for yourself!" She lived a very positive and successful life, and helped many. Another saying of hers well worth remembers is,

"Keep your face to the sunshine
and you cannot see the shadow."

A cheerful attitude, then, is what you will be aiming for, and one way of gaining this is to develop the habit of smiling. Think of the photographer. "Smile please," he says, or perhaps, "Say 'cheese'", which of course, stretches our lips into a wide grin. Somehow people usually look far more attractive when they are smiling. Yet there are certainly times when this simple action of putting a smile on our faces seems to be incredibly difficult. All the same, however we may be feeling inside, it is worth making the effort.

Teachers of small children know the value of keeping cheerful, for encouraging and jollying them along with a joke or a pleasant word is far more effective than nagging them into doing what is required of them. A smile is a very positive thing. The dictionary says it is "an expression of pleasure, amusement, affection or happiness". If we smile at small babies in prams, we usually get a smile in return. Even as adults we tend to respond to a smile by smiling back, which can immediately put us into a more friendly frame of mind.

We are told that it takes fewer muscles to smile than to frown, so if a smile becomes our natural expression, we are automatically relaxing our face muscles and so easing away tension and strain.

It was the rather enigmatic smile on the face of the famous 'Mona Lisa' painting which made it so popular, and the same is true of the picture 'The Laughing Cavalier'. When I saw the film 'Gandhi', I realised that one of the things which transformed Gandhi from an ordinary, rather insignificant little man, into the leader who was worshipped by millions, was the wonderful warmth of his smile! When watching television pictures of Mother Teresa of Calcutta, I have seen on her face the same kind of sincere and caring smile, which reveals the sort of person she is.

We can usually come across things during the course of the day which will make us smile. Sometimes the humour is quite unintentional. Children will occasionally use an incorrect word which can convey quite a different meaning. Delightful pictures may be conjured up by the following 'howlers':

> "The duke wore a scarlet cloak trimmed with vermin."

"Herrings go about the sea in shawls."
"King Henry had an abbess on his knee which made walking difficult."

There is also the story of the small child of Protestant parents who started to attend a convent school. On returning home after her first day, she horrified her mother by saying, "I told the nuns you were a prostitute, Mummy, but they only smiled."

Smiling is important both for ourselves and others. It is worth working at it, even if we feel down in the dumps and least like showing a smiling face to the world. It helps if we can practice a few smiles at ourselves in the mirror when we wake in the morning, instead of shuddering at the reflection we catch a glimpse of. Then we need to make a real effort to smile at everyone we come into contact with during the day; shop assistants, bus drivers, neighbours and so on. We may not want to talk to them, after all, no-one feels bright and chatty all the time, but just a 'Good Morning' with a smile means far more than one without. Smiles do come more easily with practice. There is also a saying that is worth keeping in mind:

"If your face wants to smile, let it.
If it doesn't, make it!"

We can help to build up our sense of humour and our ability to see the lighter side of life by reading amusing books, or watching comedy programmes on the television. Not everyone will laugh at the same sort of humour, but there is a wide range from which to choose. This is where you will have to experiment and try the different kinds until you find something which really amuses you and makes you laugh.

Most newspapers and magazines contain jokes and cartoon strips. Looking through these is an excellent way of reducing stress in doctors' or dentists' waiting rooms.

You may enjoy reading limericks, and you are probably familiar with those of Edward Lear. A typical example (though not, I think, by Lear) is:

"A fellow while dining at Crewe
Found a rather large mouse in his stew.
Said the waiter, 'Don't shout
And wave it about
Or the rest will be wanting one too.' "

It is quite amusing to try to make these up yourself, using the names of towns and fitting a rhyme around them. For example: "There was an old woman of Dover . . ., etc."

Frequently collections of the work of popular newspaper cartoonists are sold in books at Christmas time, and are very popular. It is a good idea to make a collection of your own, by cutting them out each day and pasting them in a book. Invalids would certainly appreciate such a gift. Alternatively, collect jokes and amusing stories from magazines and put them together for future reading when you need cheering up yourself.

Be sure, then, that before you continue on your way, you have made provision to carry a little humour along with you to lighten the journey. When this is done, you may proceed to door 9, for no gremlins will be lurking in *ROOM 8*. The door to *ROOM 9* carries a more sober label – '*HISTORY*'.

The Ninth Door – History

What images does the word 'history' bring to your mind? You will, perhaps, have memories of strings of dates to be learnt by heart, or lists of the kings of England in their order of succession. If so, *ROOM 9* will surprise you, for you will find nothing of the sort here. True history is not something that is as dry as dust, but is an excursion back into the living past, when we re-discover the experiences of our ancestors.

As a small child at junior school level, history was, without question, my favourite lesson. I well remember the teacher who took this subject throughout the school, a vivacious little lady with a natural gift for story telling. She would perch herself on the edge of a desk in front of the class and, as we all listened, spellbound, she would take us effortlessly back into past ages. We saw again the awed faces of the cave men when, for the first time, they accidently produced fire and realised its potential. We tramped the cold, Northern fells with Roman legions and helped them, at Hadrian's command, to erect the great wall. We roamed the seas with the fierce Vikings, hid in the fens with Hereward, sorrowed over Alfred's burnt cakes, struggled with King Charles to escape from Carisbrooke Castle, and grieved for the poor little children sent to work down the dark coal mines. This is real history; stories that are more enthralling than fiction because they are true. Before the invention of books, history was passed on to succeeding generations in this way. People would gather together, and news of battles or other great events would be told, sometimes in poetry or in song by a bard, or sometimes just in story form.

When I was old enough to progress to a grammar school, I looked forward eagerly to further adventures into history. I was sadly disappointed. History now, I found, consisted of dictated notes which we all wrote in exercise books, and then were required to memorise and reproduce in examinations. The stirring tales of old were reduced to dull recordings. I can still remember feeling that this could surely not be the same subject that had thrilled me so much in my younger years.

Now, I can see that my earlier concept of history was the right one. The one certain thing about true history is that it is never dull. It is unpredictable, and amazing things can happen at any time, both good and bad, as we have seen in our own century.

In this room, as in earlier ones, you will have freedom of choice, and will be able to select any one period of history which appeals to you, from the very earliest civilizations up to modern times. It can be history of your own, or any other country or group of countries, or indeed world history at any one particular time.

There are so many fascinating times to consider, that you will probably have difficulty in choosing. Some people like to learn more about the Ancient Egyptians and their strange beliefs, which led them to construct the pyramids; children are often attracted to prehistoric eras or the age of the dinosaurs. The Vikings, the Romans, Queen Elizabeth I, The French Revolution, and the Victorians would all be popular choices, but it will be for you to decide. History is such a wide subject, that it is more interesting to look at one part in detail, rather than to try to cover everything.

There are different ways of setting about increasing your knowledge. Your local library will, once again, be the most obvious source, and there will be plenty of books from which to make a selection. Don't necessarily look for text books only. Historical novels, biographies of famous people of the period, plays and information about the customs, dress, food and living conditions of the time could all be relevant and not difficult to read. Then there are films and documentaries, not forgetting, of course, what museums, historical buildings and art galleries can provide.

Some museums, like the one in York, offer a tour backwards through local history, in which you are transported into the past by being taken through tableaux of that particular area in earlier centuries. If your home is in the North of England, you may have an opportunity to visit Hadrian's Wall and the remains of the Roman township and fort at Vindolanda. It is well worth seeing. Should you be living in or near London, and the Victorian era was your choice, you will have ample material to study. Victorian architecture and monuments abound, and one of the many museums in Kensington presents panoramic scenes of the former glories of the British Empire. I, myself, remember the time when Empire Day, 24th May, was given great prominence. Union Jacks were flown from all public buildings, and patriotic songs were sung by the children, who would, very often, give special performances of maypole dancing and singing in the morning, and be rewarded by a half day's holiday in the afternoon. This was a typical conundrum, often posed at Victorian parties:

I sit on the rock and call for the wind,
But the storm once abated, I'm gentle and kind,
I have kings at my feet, who await but my nod
To lie down in the dust on the ground where I trod.
I'm oft seen in the world, though known but to a few,
The gentiles despise me; I'm pork to the Jew.
I never have passed but one night in the dark
And that was with Noah alone in the Ark.
My weight is 3 lbs, my length is a mile
And when you have guessed me, you'll say with a smile
That my first and my last is the boast of our Isle.

The answer, naturally enough, was "The British Empire". (The rock is Gibraltar, the three pounds refers to the Imperial weights which were avoirdupois, troyweight and pennyweight, and lines 7 and 8 to the saying that the sun never sets on the British Empire.) It is interesting to note how much public opinion has altered since those comparatively recent days, for everyone lives through a certain amount of history, and the world is continually changing.

To return to the subject of books, there is plenty of very good historical fiction, which is by no means dull. To give just a few examples, Charles Dickens' books reveal vividly many aspects of his times and, if you are discouraged by their length, you will be able to find videos of some of the better-known ones. Elizabeth Goudge brings the past to life, particularly in her novels "Green Dolphin Country", "Gentian Hill", and "The White Witch". For earlier days, Rosemary Sutcliff takes us back to the times of the Roman occupation in "The Eagle of the Ninth' and, for those who enjoy detective fiction, Ellis Peters has written a very popular series of mediaeval 'Whodunnits' set in the time of the wars between Stephen and Matilda in the 12th century.

Don't always feel that you must keep strictly to your chosen period. You should concentrate mainly on this, but if you find other snippets of history in your home area which interest you, by all means investigate them. Check television and radio programmes for historical features, and do not neglect stately homes in your locality which may be open to the public. These can reveal many historical treasures, and there are usually guides to give you the details you require.

Recently, a company known as "Past Times" has opened shops in various parts of the country selling reproductions or small models of items in common use during past centuries. These are quite reasonably priced, and it is certainly worth browsing through the shop if you discover one.

Because there is so much on offer for you in this room, it is not possible to give you detailed guidance. You must just take your time and sift through the various materials until you find where your interests lie. To become immersed in past history is a wonderful form of relief from present day problems, and you will find it a relief to have times when, by dipping into a book, or compiling a scrap collection, or wandering round an ancient building, you can re-create the atmosphere of a long ago age.

You will not, though, be able to elude the ever-watchful gremlin, who sees no useful purpose at all for this room.

Gremlin: "It's boring!"

ANSWER: How can it be, when it is concerned with real people and life and death struggles of the past? There is so much here, that there must be something to interest everyone.

Gremlin: "What use is all this raking up of past history? It can't be altered now."

ANSWER: We learn from what happened in the past, and it helps us to understand ourselves better.

Gremlin: "Who cares about people who have been dead and gone for ages?

ANSWER: They are our ancestors, and what we are now depended on what they did then. We need to know about them.

Once the gremlin has given up and gone, you will have to work out how best to include some history in your programme; just occasionally, perhaps, by an excursion here and there, or time spent in selecting suitable books to read when you have the odd half hour. Write down the particular things which will interest you most and, of course, the special period with which you would like to become more familiar.

After this, you are free to continue on your way. The door you will reach next is inscribed 'SPORT'.

The Tenth Door – Sport

It may be that you have stopped on reaching this door. You are possibly thinking, 'Oh no; I've come this far, but sport is just not for me'. There is no need to worry. If you are elderly, in poor health, or simply not a sports-loving person, you will find an alternative route is available once you have entered the room. Look for a side door marked '*SPECTATOR SPORT*'. The purpose of *ROOM 10* is not necessarily to improve your health through exercise, though this would be a bonus, but to provide you with pleasure and a contrast to all your intellectual studies.

As in so many of the rooms through which you have already travelled, 'sport' can describe a multitude of activities, and, once more, you will be called upon to make a choice. For some of you, this will present no difficulty at all. If you are already devoted to football, tennis, ice skating, swimming or golf, your way forward is clear, and you simply have to indulge in your favourite sport whenever the occasion or the opportunity arises.

For others, there will be a need to look carefully at the varied types of sports on offer, and a challenge to attempt something new. Remember that in all sports there is a wonderful chance to meet with your fellows for a shared pleasure, and to work either as a team or in friendly competition.

Here are a few examples of the different categories:

INDOOR: darts, ten-pin bowling, roller skating, snooker, billiards, badminton

WATER: sail-boarding, yachting, ice-skating, swimming

TEAM: cricket, football (both Association and Rugby), hockey, netball, bowls

AGGRESSIVE: judo, karate, boxing, wrestling

COMPETITIVE: tennis, golf, athletics

SPECTATOR: dog and horse racing, most of the team and competitive sports, including American football, and big events such as the Commonwealth and Olympic Games.

This is only a selection of the options available for you. You will, doubtless, know of others that could be added. To take an active part in some will obviously be possible only if you are young, fit and reasonably agile; others, such as darts, golf, bowls and ten-pin bowling, can be enjoyed at almost any age, and at varying degrees of competence. The benefits of participation are plain to see, so do consider making the attempt.

Spectator sports fall into two divisions; those which you will see live, by going to the football ground or race track, and those which can be viewed on the television or followed on the radio. Much pleasure can be derived from both. If you would not describe yourself as a 'sporting type', and have, in the past, always sighed and switched channels whenever sport in any guise has featured on the television, now is the time for you to make a change, and to select a particular sport which you will follow. There is sufficient variety for you to be able to find one that will offer you at least some degree of pleasure. If you consider cricket to be boring, there is no point in sitting through a lengthy commentary which has little meaning for you. Try something completely different. There are some who would not dream of going to a football match, but will thoroughly enjoy watching American Football on television, because they find the antics of the players and their grotesque protective clothing hilarious. My aunt, a sweet and gentle old lady, loved to watch wrestling, and many who are not normally interested in tennis, are glued to their screens during the Wimbledon tournaments. The Olympic Games make compulsive viewing for hundreds of people, and snooker championships, ice skating, and winter sports events also attract large audiences.

What you will be required to do, then, in this room, is to select a sport which you will either go to watch, view regularly on the television, or in which you will participate yourself. You will discover that, even if you start out with just a tiny spark of interest, your addiction to it will grow, until it has become yet another source of pleasure and enrichment.

Although the resident gremlin will still be muttering away about your complete indifference to anything even remotely connected with sport, even he can hardly fail to see that the minimum requirement of watching an occasional sports programme, is within the reach of everyone. As those who do enjoy sport will simply brush aside his complaints about games being a waste of time, he will have little influence on anyone in this room, and can be disregarded.

Resolve, therefore, to make some provision henceforth for sport in your life and, having done this, you will be ready to leave *ROOM 10* and try the next door, on which is written, *'LITERATURE'*.

The Eleventh Door – Literature

You will find the eleventh room very different again from all the others. It resembles an enormous indoor garden, with winding paths leading off in all directions. Whichever one you take will bring you, after a while, into a pleasant and secluded bower with mossy banks and shady trees, where you may rest for a while and take your ease. In some of these small retreats you will find a rustic seat beside a quiet lake, in others you will be surrounded by masses of beautiful flowers and, in a few, there will be a dramatic background of towering mountain peaks and cascading waterfalls. They represent the pleasures you will find by escaping, for a time, into the world of literature.

It is a boundless world. So many books have been written since the invention of printing, that it would be impossible to estimate their number. However, in this room you will only be considering books that are regarded as good literature, because they have been well written and have remained popular over a considerable period of time. Some books have a brief notoriety and are then forgotten; others, written centuries ago, are still best sellers. It is quality that counts, and books like these are always worth reading.

On looking back over your journey, you will see what an important part books have played. Time and again, you have been referred to the library as the source of information. In most of the other rooms you have selected one particular line of study. Here it will be different, for you can browse at leisure, and read as much or as little as you please of any one author. If you have poor sight or, for any reason, find reading tedious, you will be able to choose books in large print or, alternatively, story cassettes of many well-known books.

If you are not a great reader and most of the classics are unknown territory to you, I would certainly recommend just dipping into some of them and browsing around until you find something that holds your interest. You are not expected to plough your way through a long and dreary tome, in order to add to the total of books you have read. Your aim is certainly to cover new ground, but also to find pleasure in the process. If you have already made the acquaintance of the more popular classics, then you will need to widen your field and try new authors, or switch to poetry or plays.

I was very fortunate, as a child, to have free access to books of all kinds. My parents' tastes differed widely, as the contents of our bookcase revealed, and I had a teacher aunt who saw that I was supplied with literature which she considered suitable for my educational needs. I enjoyed the usual children's classics, and also sampled various types of adult literature at random, only dimly understanding much of it, but finding it fascinating to wander into this unknown and exciting world of books. My mother had been given a most beautifully illustrated "Pilgrim's Progress" as a Sunday School prize, and this became a special favourite, though I had to skip over most of the longer words and outdated phraseology.

Reading is a great joy, and books can become real friends. The test of a good book is to find that you want to go back to it over and over again. Many can be read and enjoyed, then returned to the library and forgotten, but a book that is special is one that you will wish to possess for yourself. The well-known classics are those which are not only skilfully written, but have some quality in the stories they tell that catches our imagination, so that we feel we are actually seeing the events that are taking place. We admire some books because of their beautiful composition and the perfection of language. Spoken English reached its peak at the time of Shakespeare, and he was able to employ words as an artist uses colour.

The same is true of the Authorised Version of the Bible. Many of its passages can be enjoyed for the sheer and almost musical beauty of their vocabulary. Language, however, is constantly changing to meet the needs of each age. New words are added; others alter their meaning or become obsolete. Consequently, in order to ensure the correct understanding of books such as the Bible, modern translations have been brought out, which are deplored by some because of the inferior quality of the contemporary English in which they are written.

Beautiful though the original works are, though, it would be easy to misunderstand some of the passages completely, without the help of a more modern version. In the Anglican prayer book, for instance, the word 'prevent' in the prayer "Lord, we pray that thy grace may always prevent and follow us", means 'go before', not 'stop'. 'Comfort' in the old sense, was 'to come alongside to strengthen', not as we might suppose 'to console', and the original meaning of 'silly', was 'simple' or 'guileless'. Thee and thou instead of you, were in everyday use in earlier times, whereas to us, they seem clumsy and outdated, though they persisted in dialect, especially in the North, until comparatively recently. We do not always realise how much our language has changed until we look at writings of Elizabethan times and find them extremely difficult to decipher, for many of the words seem quite different from those in use now.

Until quite recently, an alternative spelling of the verb to show was 'shew'. Curiously enough, some of the old English forms are still preserved in American speech. They have retained the word 'gotten' (e.g. He has gotten himself a bride) and they will say 'He dove into the water', whereas we would now say 'dived'. It is interesting to note that the bird called a dove was given its name from the Old English dufedoppe, which means a diving bird, perhaps because of the way it dives through the air. If we go right back to Anglo-Saxon times, English has the appearance of a completely foreign language. These are a few lines from the ancient poem "Beowulf", thought to have been written in the eighth century:

> Nu is se raed gelang
> Eft oet the anum. Eard git ne const,
> Frecne stowe, thaer thu finden miht
> Felasinnigne secg: sec gif thu dyrre!

A translation of this (by Gavin Bone) is:

> Once again our hope
> Rests with you to upbear:
> As yet you know not the haunt where you may cope
> With the paramount evil: seek if you dare!

If the evolution of language interests you, it is worthwhile investing in an etymological dictionary (Chambers' for example) which, as well as their meaning, will give the derivation of words.

Should you be wondering where to begin your search among this great treasure-store of literature, I would suggest your trying an anthology, which will give you sample excerpts from many books or poems. These are often produced for children, in order to introduce them to gems of literature, so once more, the children's library would be a good starting point. Having discovered a likely author, you could then go on to look for the complete works.

Do make a point of reading the most popular of the children's classics which have stood the test of time, if you did not have the opportunity to do so in your own childhood. They have remained firm favourites not only because they are unique stories, each with a special enchantment of its own, but because they embody deep truths which can also be appreciated by adult readers. Everyone should be familiar with the following:

"The Wind in the Willows" by Kenneth Grahame
"Alice in Wonderland" by Lewis Carroll
"Peter Pan" by J.M. Barrie
"The Mowgli Stories" by Rudyard Kipling

"The Water Babies" by Charles Kingsley
"Treasure Island" by R.L. Stevenson
"The Chronicles of Narnia" by C.S. Lewis
The stories of Hans Andersen (which include, of course,
"The Little Mermaid" and "The Ugly Duckling").

In children's literature you will also find famous legends of our own country, such as King Arthur and his knights, and tales of Robin Hood. These have a historical foundation entwined with folk lore. You will come across King Arthur again in poetry (Tennyson's "Idylls of the King") and in adult fiction, such as Mary Stewart's "The Crystal Cave".

Even if you have never read the books, you will be familiar with the names of Jane Eyre, Lorna Doone and the Scarlet Pimpernel and, if you have not yet made their closer acquaintance, they are certainly to be recommended.

Sometimes people are introduced to an author by seeing his stories brought to life on the television. Presentations of "The Forsyte Saga", "Barchester Towers" and "Wuthering Heights" sent people to the works of Galsworthy, Trollope and the Brontes, and many who had felt the writings of Russian authors would be far above their heads, changed their minds after seeing the film versions of "Dr Zhivago" or "War and Peace".

Try looking for familiar titles along the classical literature shelves in bookshops. There is no need to purchase a book unless you are sure you will enjoy it. Once you have a possible author and title, seek it out again in the library. What an enormous asset a library can be! "Dip and delve" might be your policy for a while, until you find a writer whose books you can read with pleasure. I remember, as a child, the thrill of discovering a new author who was 'on my wavelength', so that, having revelled in one of his books, I could go on expectantly to however many others were still in store. This pleasure can be repeated throughout our lives, and *ROOM 11* is offering you these very opportunities.

If you are already an avid reader, you will need little

encouragement to give time in your life to books. There is still the temptation, though, of being drawn exclusively to the same type of literature whenever we look for reading material. If you are prone to seek out only romances, or science fiction, or detective or spy stories, try to vary this a little. When collecting a batch of books from the library, ensure that one is different from your normal choice; an autobiography, perhaps, or something written by an author who is quite new to you.

Never be satisfied with your literary achievements. If most of the classics are familiar to you, try more modern writers, consider taking a course in English literature, or joining a poetry circle, or a writers' group. In this way you would gain by the opinions of others, and add to your own knowledge and pleasure. Writing poetry is a skill that is dormant in many. Perhaps you possess it too. It is worth trying and, as in so much else, talent is improved by practice. Look for biographies of the more famous poets and writers. They often make very interesting reading.

There are likely to be several gremlins on the prowl, for they despise books and would be delighted to lure you away from them.

Gremlin: "You have always found reading rather heavy going, so why make life more difficult for yourself?"

ANSWER: There is no need to go to difficult and complicated books. We can find pleasure in simple tales written for children, or listen to stories on cassettes.

Gremlin: "Reading is a bore."

ANSWER: It is no such thing. We choose books which will thrill, amuse, move, or divert us. Good literature takes us out of ourselves, and is designed for our pleasure.

Gremlin: "Too much reading is bad for your eyes."

ANSWER: This is an old wives tale. We may tire our eyes by reading in a poor light, or by not wearing glasses if we are short sighted, but eyesight is not harmed by usage.

Gremlin: "How can you make friends with people if you are always buried in a book?"

ANSWER: No-one is going to spend the whole day reading; it will just be one of many activities. The knowledge gained by it can be shared and discussed with others, enabling us to contribute to and enjoy interesting conversations. It will help us to feel more at ease with others and will, therefore, assist in building up friendships.

Do not be in a hurry to leave this room. It is a restful place and has much of value to offer you. However, when you feel ready to continue the journey, you should make your way through the door at the farthest end. This will lead you once more into the corridor, with another door ahead marked '*MUSIC*'.

The Twelfth Door – Music

This is, once more, a circular room, with many doors leading from it into comfortable lounges or small theatres, each of which will be devoted to a different type of music. It has been truly said that one man's music is another man's noise, and there are, indeed, many interpretations of what may be termed music. A dictionary would probably define it as sound that is pleasing to the ear, but the purpose of music is not only to give us relaxation and enjoyment, but to enable us to express a greater depth of feeling than is possible in mere words. This is why music or singing plays an important part in most of the world's religions. It is a form of creative art, like poetry or painting, and we can either produce music for ourselves by playing an instrument, or derive pleasure from just listening to it.

Music appears to be unique to mankind, for the animal world seems to have no use for it. We discover music, though, in some form or another, in every race and culture and from very early times. It may be merely a rhythmic drumbeat, or hand clapping, or queer discordant piping on reed instruments, but music has played a part in religious ceremonies, wars, tribal rituals, weddings, funerals and times of rejoicing all through the centuries.

It has a vital role to play in our lives, and I think we all probably have inherited a need for some kind of music. The baby is soothed to sleep by a lullaby, the small child sings nursery rhymes, and we learn the old country folk ballads, or hum or whistle the popular songs of the moment which we hear on the television or radio. Musical stage productions become successful because of their tunefulness, and people remember the more lively choruses. When we are happy, we feel the urge to sing, and there are plenty of songs in our heritage from which to choose.

I can recall my mother singing numbers from the old Music Halls as she did the housework, and we would join in with "Daisy, Daisy", or "Let's all go down the Strand". Father liked to sing in the bathroom. There is something about a bathroom which seems to encourage singing; perhaps a certain resonance which can be produced more easily there than in other rooms of the house, or the privacy which induces an uninhibited performance. Father's favourite song always began "This is the admiral's story. . .", though I cannot remember now what the admiral had to tell.

Musical instruments, to accompany singing or chanting, have a very long history. I suppose the earliest types would be simple drums, cymbals, rattles or horns, together with reed pipes and whistles. Stringed instruments would have evolved later, and rhythm probably preceded melody. Rhythmic beating or clapping would stimulate dancers to keep time, help rowers to regulate the dip of their oars, or encourage weary soldiers to continue a long march. In Africa, today, country people still sing as they work or row down the river, and the drum plays an important part in their ceremonial occasions. Modern song groups rely heavily on this hypnotic and rhythmic pulse beat which characterises their form of music.

The value of music in keeping boredom at bay when engaged in monotonous duties, was proved during the last war, when factories found that production went up considerably if they relayed continuous, cheerful music to their employees. Supermarkets often use the same procedure of background music, in the hope that it will induce in their customers a relaxed frame of mine, so that they will linger and, perhaps, make more purchases.

In ancient times music was considered to possess magical powers and, in the myths, we hear of Pan playing on his pipes, and Orpheus his lute. In the tale of the Pied Piper, it was his music which lured the rats to their doom, and the children to leave their homes. Children find a great sense of achievement in being able to produce music, even if it is only from a tin whistle or a comb and paper.

Sometimes, one particular instrument will be characteristic of a country. Scotland has its bagpipes, Ireland the harp, and the Welsh express their love of music in singing.

All the various types of music are offered to you in this room, and you will be asked to make a choice of two. The first will be that to which you feel the most attracted; the second, a form of music to which, normally, you would never be inclined to listen. It is a mistake, I think, to dismiss certain categories out of hand, when we have never seriously given them a hearing. We cannot know whether or not we will enjoy something, until we have actually experienced it. Taste must sometimes be acquired, and we can miss a great deal in life by being afraid to experiment. If, therefore, you never listen to anything but classical music, or if, on the other hand, your musical acquaintance to date has been an exclusive diet of Radio 1 or Radio 2, try occasionally to make a change. It would be wiser not to go from one extreme to the other. 'Pop' music fans, for instance, would probably find light classical music, or Country and Western more acceptable than a concert of Chamber music.

Some of the categories available are:

Modern "Pop" groups

Blues, Rock, or Heavy Metal

Traditional Jazz

Country and Western, and Folk

Ballet music

Popular music from films, shows, operettas and comic operas

Choral works

Opera

Light Classical

Serious Classical (Chamber and Orchestral music)

When you have chosen two from the list, you will be able to find the areas allotted to them, and you must then decide how much time you can give to each. No doubt, you will wish to spend longer on your favourite type, and this will be allowed, so long as you are prepared to devote a little attention to the second. You may well find, to your surprise, that as you grow more accustomed to this different form of music, you will be more appreciative of it. You might even, eventually, change your order of preference.

Before you leave *ROOM 12*, there will be yet another challenge for you. Why not learn to play an instrument yourself? Perhaps you already have some slight skill as a pianist, on which you could improve. If you are musically inclined, a recorder is not a difficult instrument to master, and you might consider taking an instruction course. Do you enjoy singing? Then why not join a local choir or operatic society? If these suggestions do not seem practicable, there are, perhaps, concerts you could attend, or musical appreciation classes. Do think about all these options.

There is no doubt that some aspects of this room will be entirely pleasing. You will be able to relax while you listen, for part of the time at least, to the kind of music which you most enjoy. Nonetheless, the gremlin will be impatient:

Gremlin: "You are not musical, so this room is a waste of time. You could be getting on with the journey."
ANSWER: Music is a vital part of life. It will give us renewed energy for the journey.
Gremlin: "What is the point of listening to music you don't like?"
ANSWER: We need to know why other people like it and to try to understand it. It will help us, in turn, to understand them.
Gremlin: "All this lazing around will get you nowhere."

ANSWER: On the contrary, relaxation is very necessary and music can be a very enriching experience.

When you leave this room, you will be encouraged to learn that you are now not far from the end of your journey. The door to *ROOM 13* is inscribed '*TIME-TABLE*'.

The Thirteenth Door – Timetable

On opening this door, you will find yourself in a very small room containing only a table and chair. On the table, paper and a pen are laid out for you. You will need to spend only a short time here for, having come successfully through the twelve preceding rooms and been given tasks and assignments in each, your objective now is to fit all of these into whatever time is at your disposal.

Time is a curious thing. For many lonely people, an hour can seem to drag on interminably, and a whole day be an eternity. To others, the clock rushes relentlessly on, as they desperately strive to meet a deadline. If we are late for an appointment the minutes race past; if we are waiting in the cold for a train or bus, they will crawl with tantalising slowness. There is a puzzle about time, which goes:

"Time flies you cannot they fly so fast."

It appears, at first, to make no sense, until you realise that it is referring to flies as insects, and properly punctuated, it reads:

"Time flies you cannot; they fly so fast."

The fact remains, though, that the amount of time you need to fill will be variable, according to your own circumstances. If you are retired, or for any other reason do not have paid employment, you will, once any necessary shopping, cooking and housework have been done, find much of the day is left over. For others, there will only be evenings, weekends and holiday periods to fill. Naturally, most people who are lonely will have an excess of spare time, for it is the empty hours of boredom which make loneliness such a miserable experience.

By now you will have collected a formidable load of tasks and undertakings and you are probably wondering how all of them can possibly be integrated into your life. It is essential to draw up some kind of schedule. I had a neighbour, some time ago, who had an extremely full life. She took in paying guests, and coped single-handed with all the cooking and cleaning involved. Yet, despite this, she could always spare the time for a leisurely chat or a cheery word. When asked how she managed, she would always reply, "Ah, I have a schedule, you see." She knew exactly what her work entailed and kept to a strict timetable, daily, weekly and monthly, including in it periods of free time for her own very necessary relaxation.

This sort of planning is now required of you, and is the purpose of this room. No further tasks will be added, for your journey is almost at an end, but before you can put into practice all you have learned, some sort of order has to be established.

First, you should write down a list of all the activities assigned to you, starting with those of *ROOM 1*. Put them into groups; those that must be carried out daily, those weekly, and those which can be undertaken occasionally when the right opportunity presents itself. Then, the amount of time you can give to each has to be decided. Your aim is to fit all of them into whatever free moments you have, making sure that you have completely filled each day. Some of these activities, as you have discovered, are designed for relaxation and pleasure, but there must be no vacuum remaining. All your time should be accounted for in one way or another.

This will be a very personal and individual plan and will need careful thought, so don't be tempted to rush. Your timetable is all-important. Naturally, rules are made to be broken, so there may be a day when you have an unexpected invitation, or feel the urge to spend a little time in the sunshine instead of poring over a book. By all means, in such cases, depart briefly from your schedule, but return to it as soon as you can, and use it as a guide.

What you are aiming to do is to fill up completely all your waking hours, because it is aimless drifting and boredom which lead to loneliness and dissatisfaction in life. It is possible to be lonely even if you live with your family, but usually the risk is not so great then, because, whether you wish it or not, you are bound to become involved, to a certain extent, in the lives of others. For those living alone, the problem of loneliness is ever present and, for them, it is essential to learn the skills of coping with and finding contentment in a solitary life. The strategies you have gleaned in travelling through the foregoing rooms will build up, I am convinced, into the answer you seek. It is now up to you to put them into practice.

Think and plan carefully, because this is the scheme which can lay the foundation for your future happiness. Then, when your timetable is fully completed, take it with you, together with your passport, as you prepare to enter the final room which is entitled '*JOURNEY'S END*'.

The Fourteenth Door – Journey's End

This small room is the ante-chamber to your new way of life. In it you are going to think over all you have learned, both about yourself and the world around you. When you emerge into that world, you will find it very different from the one from which you escaped by venturing on this journey.

Do not expect, though, that no further effort is required of you. The life that is opening before you now is rich in wonderful opportunities of fulfilment and happiness, but these are not going to empty themselves into your lap. They are there to be won, and you are now well equipped to gain them, but each has to be sought and earned.

You are in the same position as the Pilgrim Fathers, who, having fled from their narrow, unhappy and restricted life in England, found themselves, after a weary and perilous journey across the Atlantic, in the wonderful 'New World' of America. Once there, however, they had to tackle all the hazards of an unfamiliar climate and unfriendly Indians, and to build up homesteads, plant crops and rear their children in virgin territory, completely different from anything they had known before. Nonetheless, it was far preferable to the life they had left behind, and the prosperous American nation of today testifies to how well they succeeded. It was their courage and determination to overcome any obstacles which carried them through and also the hardships of the journey over those stormy seas, which built up their strength. You, too, were brave enough to tackle this long and arduous escape route, and you, too, will find that your passage through it has changed and strengthened you, and given you new insights on how to cope with the problems of life.

Another well-known journey from slavery and misery in the hope of finding a life of freedom, was that made by the Israelites escaping from Egypt. After long wanderings in a desert wilderness, they, too, found happiness in a new land. They did not just walk into a paradise of ease and comfort, but the hardships of their journey had prepared them to overcome the opposition they at first encountered, and to achieve their aim of becoming a great nation in much the same way as those first American settlers so many centuries later.

Do not, therefore, expect that as you walk out of the final exit of this escape route, you will find a crowd of potential friends all waiting to greet you and sweep you for ever away from your former life of loneliness. This achievement is possible, but you have yet to win it. Throughout this long journey, your efforts have been preparing you for this very task, and you are not now the same person as you were when you commenced your pilgrimage. You thus have every chance of success, for you will find yourself far more self-confident and better prepared to deal with the threat of loneliness.

Your greatest desire is, obviously, to find friends and companionship, so before you set out, this room will remind you of the right and wrong ways to set about it. You will remember that, at the start of the journey, you were specifically warned NOT to seek out friends. Over-eagerness will so often drive away those who might otherwise have befriended us. Friendship, like a plant, has to grow naturally and, above all, slowly.

As a child, I was extremely shy and withdrawn, so that I seldom had playmates of my own age. I can remember a well-meaning aunt taking me to the park and pointing out a group of children, all strangers to me, who were playing happily near by. "Go up to them and ask if you can join in", she urged. I can recall how horrified I was at the mere suggestion. I instinctively knew that to intrude like this would be wrong. It is an unwritten law of childhood that you do not gatecrash in this way. It is much the same in adult life. You cannot force or bribe anyone to accept you as a friend.

Sometimes the first step would be to enjoy the company of a cat or dog or other domestic pet. These often provide a means of introduction to fellow pet owners. In following the timetable you have drawn up for yourself, you will undoubtedly be brought into contact with others. In the course of conversations and shared tasks or pleasures, opportunities for friendship could arise. Deal with these carefully, and remember to observe these rules:

1. If invited to have a cup of tea or coffee, do not stay for longer than about an hour, unless pressed to extend your visit. Not everyone has unlimited time at their disposal.

2. If people call on you, make them welcome, but don't reproach them for not coming more often.

3. Never monopolise a conversation. If is more important to listen than to speak. Show an interest in your companion's news before relating your own.

4. Except in cases of real emergency, do not call on any but really intimate friends without an invitation.

5. Do not make constant phone calls, unless you know these will be welcome.

6. Do not go on at great length about your own ailments or a recent operation. The personal and intimate details are of interest only to you, and many people would find them distasteful.

7. Try to avoid gossip or derogatory talk about others, and never, under any circumstances, betray a confidence.

8. Always be ready to offer a listening ear, sympathy and encouragement.

There is a little rhyme which aptly sums up all this advice:

> I went out to seek a friend
> But could not find one there.
> Then I went out to BE a friend,
> And friends were everywhere.

There is no door at the end of this room; just a turnstile where your passport will be stamped to show that you have completed the journey. You will emerge into the sunshine beyond, happy and confident that you now have many interests and know that you are able to make the best of your abilities. Keep your passport always with you; the resolution contained within it will be an excellent guide for the future.

Congratulations on successfully completing a difficult course!

Go forward with a smile to your new, fuller and happier life.

Useful Addresses

THE PORTIA TRUST, Workspace, Maryport, Cumbria, CA15 8NF (publishes a magazine, 'Future Friends' for lonely people)

DEPRESSIVES ASSOCIATED, P.O. Box 5, Castletown, Portland, Dorset, DT5 1BQ

DEPRESSIVES ANONYMOUS, 36 Chestnut Ave., Beverley, N. Humberside, HU17 9QU (both these Associations have pen-friend schemes)

NATIONAL WOMEN'S REGISTER, 245 Warwick Rd., Solihull, W. Midlands, B92 7AH (local groups for discussion and friendship)

NATIONAL ASSOCIATION OF WOMEN'S CLUBS, 5 Vernon Rise, London, WC1X 9CP (over 600 local clubs)

NATIONAL FEDERATIONS OF 18 PLUS GROUPS, (for men and women 18–30) Nicholson House, Old Court Road, Newent, Glos. GL18 1AG (local groups for weekend sporting and social activities)

CONTACT, (for isolated elderly people) 15 Henrietta Street, Covent Garden, London, WC2E 8QH

CRUSE, Cruse House, 126 Sheen Road, Richmond, Surrey, TW9 1VR (for widows and widowers)

NATIONAL ASSOCIATION OF WIDOWS, 1st Floor, Neville House, 14 Waterloo St., Birmingham, BT 5TX

SOCIETY OF TEACHERS OF THE ALEXANDER TECHNIQUE, 3B Albert Court, Kensington Gore, London SW7

WORLD WIDE TAPE TALK, 35 The Gardens, W. Harrow, Middlesex, HA1 4HE (links those wishing to communicate by tape)

R.S.P.B. (Royal Society for the protection of birds) The Lodge, Sandy, Beds, SG19 2DL

OXFAM, 274 Banbury Road, Oxford, OX2 7DZ

PAST TIMES, Guildford House, Hayle, Cornwall, TR27 6PT (shops in London, Cambridge, Chichester, Exeter, Oxford and York)

'YOURS', (magazine for older folk who are young at heart) Apex House, Oundle Road, Peterborough, PE2 9NP

AGE CONCERN, Astral House, 1268 London Road, London SW16 4EJ